Lawrence N. Greenleaf

King Sham, and other Atrocities in Verse

Including a Humorous History of the Pike's Peak Excitement

Lawrence N. Greenleaf

King Sham, and other Atrocities in Verse
Including a Humorous History of the Pike's Peak Excitement

ISBN/EAN: 9783743328624

Manufactured in Europe, USA, Canada, Australia, Japa

Cover: Foto ©ninafisch / pixelio.de

Manufactured and distributed by brebook publishing software (www.brebook.com)

Lawrence N. Greenleaf

King Sham, and other Atrocities in Verse

King Sham,

and

Other Atrocities in Verse;

including a

Humorous History

of the

Pike's Peak Excitement.

by

LAWRENCE N. GREENLEAF.

NEW YORK:

PUBLISHED BY HURD AND HOUGHTON,

459 Broome Street.

1868.

Entered according to Act of Congress, in the year 1868, by
HURD AND HOUGHTON,
in the Clerk's Office of the District Court for the Southern District of New York.

RIVERSIDE, CAMBRIDGE:
STEREOTYPED AND PRINTED BY
H. O. HOUGHTON AND COMPANY.

PREFACE.

MANY of the pieces in this collection were first made public under the *nom de plume* of "Peter Pun-ever."

Though the fact of their having "gone the rounds" and "stood the press" might argue their popularity, not till an author is fairly "under cover" are the critics in "full cry!" Readers, on the contrary, are expected to be "full of laugh"—a state of hilarity, according to the old adage, so highly conducive to corpulency, that it must necessarily involve questions of considerable weight. The division of literature into "Solid Reading" and "Reading for the Solid," may yet be rendered imperative.

Leaving all such speculations, however, to those philosophically inclined, with a firm conviction that prefaces, generally speaking, are unnecessary inflictions, and that one who, in this enlightened age, knowingly, willfully, and maliciously commits "poetry," can have no reasonable excuse to offer, I subside with the following (the idea having originated with Foote, it appeals the more directly to the understanding) : —

I've taken off all sorts of folks, 'tis right
That I should take myself off — so, good-night.

CONTENTS.

The Ice-breaker	7
King Sham; a Hit at the Times	9
The Seventh Son of a Seventh Son	31
Response to a Toast	35
Oysters, fried in Crumbs	36
On Youthful Linguists	37
Verses and Reverses	38
Ned Brown; or, the Biter bit	41
The Office Seeker	45
The Spreading Rumor	47
Bachelor Babbitt	48
Sold!	50
A Logical Conclusion	51
Scandal and Tea	51
Pike's Peakers of '59	52
The Turkey War	64
Shovels and Picks; or, the Model Superintendent	70
A Query	75
The Cheese Box	76
The In-spired Author	77
Decidedly Sheepish!	78
Youth — divested of Sentiment	79
Epigram on Gormandizer	80

Jesting and Digesting	81
On the Defensive	82
Very Chagrining!	83
In for Fun	84
On the Prospect of a Draft in New York City	85
On Hand!	87
The Mystery Solved	90
A Dubious Command	92
Quips, Quirks, and Quibbles	93
The Skeleton in an Amour	96
Prices Current	100

SERIOUS AND OCCASIONAL PIECES.

Shades and Gleams	105
Columbus	107
Remembrance	120
The Soft Answer	121
The Taunt	122
O You may sing of the Rosy Wine	123
The War	124
The Prophet of our Dreams	125
Poem for the Fourth of July	127
Poem for St. John's Day	131
Notes	140

THE ICE-BREAKER.

OFT in the still and gloomy hour of night,
When not a star or planet greets the sight,
When all seems drear — before us in the dark
The little fire-fly sheds its starry spark.
So, I, now that the shining lights of song
Withdraw awhile their presence from the throng,
Would seize the moment to invoke the Nine,
And with the lightest verses strive to shine!
Good counsel gives my Muse for times like these —
Instead of " Please to write," says, " Write to please."
Ah! what will please? I often gravely ask,
And then with trembling hand begin my task.
If you are curious, listen to my cue;
You sue for fun, 'tis fun that I pursue.
For I contend, a line in mirthful strain
Is worth a score of sonnets to Matilda Jane.
And he whose pen doth make the laugh go round,
May not be great or with the laurel crowned,
Yet 'mong his friends, who pile the praise on thick,
Pass for a "lion" or a "perfect brick!"
Perhaps a word, a thought, awakes my Muse,
I grasp my pen and penetration use;
Description fails; alas! that power I lack, —
Pegasus rears and throws me from his back.
Don't laugh, my friends, that I received a fall,
Poetic lays are much esteemed by all.

I raise my eyes, and then myself I raise,
Pegasus paws the ground, I pause and gaze;
Then grasp his mane, the main thing I may say,
Leap on his back, and onward urge my way
Straight o'er the turnpike road which leads to Fun,
And, like John Gilpin, go upon the run.
I write in vain, — that is, in humorous vein, —
Or strain your patience with some mirthful strain!
My hand is on my brow, my steed doth browse
On all the puns the jovial Muse allows.
Remember, they are scarce these latter days,
We have to fetch them a tremendous ways!
I write a line — erase it — "there's the rub!"
See how the punster bites his pencil nub.
How thick the dents with thoughts identified —
Come, laughing MOMUS, o'er my verse preside!

KING SHAM.

A HIT AT THE TIMES.

THE petty despot may control a state,
   A vaster realm ambitious potentate;
But greater still the subject of my rhymes,
Who claims adherents in all lands and climes —
The great King Sham, how wondrous is his sway!
Kings, princes, priests, and people throng the way
To Humbug Palace, and allegiance own
To him who sits upon a bogus throne;
Who wears paste diamonds in his plated crown,
Whose royal purple is a shoddy gown!
Whose long ambrosial locks (so poets sing)
Adorned the peasant ere they graced the king!
Whose beard was gray, until a liquid dye
Transformed it black as midnight's starless sky.
The flush upon his cheek — a subterfuge,
Two coats of "Lilly White" and one of Rouge!
The pearly teeth his parted lips expose
Are artificial, and — so is his nose!

Strange that to him mankind should bend the knee,
Deceit his law, and Humbug his decree;
Whose honeyed words conceal a purpose vile;
Whose smile, so winning, is a tempter's smile.

Whose shriek of anguish is ecstatic joy;
His look of pity, hate that would destroy.
Gentle his tones, when anger doth prevail;
His tears are gladness, and his laugh a wail.
He looks most hopeful though his heart despair,
And breathes a blasting curse in seeming prayer.

View Humbug Palace with distrustful eyes,
Whose marble walls in stately grandeur rise;
Profuse in ornament, above, below; —
What dazzling splendor, and what gorgeous show!
All glare and glitter, tinsel and veneer;
King Sham's abode — of course there's gammon here!
Those marble walls, alas, are refuse brick,
O'erspread with mastic scarce two inches thick!
With cunning skill the massive blocks are traced,
Apparent veins, sharp zigzags interlaced.
From base to dome, or cornice, cap or sill,
Where'er we turn, a splendid mockery still!
Above the lofty tower, to tatters torn,
There waves a banner, blazoned with a Horn!
A fitting symbol, though he talks most chaste,
In which his actions may be rightly placed!

His council hall the Muse shall open fling;
There, on his bogus throne, reclines the king.
Behold the flashy splendor of his court,
Where cunning knaves and hypocrites resort;
Astrologers, impostors, lottery-schemers,
Shrewd fortune-tellers, and clairvoyant-dreamers;
Keen operators, getters-up of swindles,
For instance — Stock, which down to nothing dwindles!

Pickpockets, sharpers of the *genus* quack,
Mock auctioneers, one driver of a hack!
Sleek "thimble-riggers," slippery as an eel,
With "pigeon-droppers" close upon their heel.
Some pious knaves and fashionable preachers;
Wire-pulling demagogues, deceitful creatures;
Dishonest tradesmen; few, if any, Quakers;
Note-forgers, and suspicious sausage-makers!
With "bounty-jumpers," quite a late invention;
And scores of others that I cannot mention.
A few there were, of managers and actors;
The devil knows how many of contractors!
Adepts in cunning, marvels of deceit;—
Such are the courtiers cringing at his feet.

Bogus the coin and counterfeit the bills,
With which his followers' craft his treasury fills.
His court physician you have heard about,
"Whose sands of life have nearly all run out."
Thus swallows down, to cure his various ills,
Empiric nostrums, Purgum's patent pills!
But last of all, the very climax capping,
Is his religion — modern spirit-rapping!

Oft to his feasts his retinue repair —
Behold, the fearless Muse conducts you there.
When once within his spacious banquet hall,
Observe the paintings on the gaudy wall:
Among the rest, on which your glances strike,
Bless me, a Rubens, Titian, and Vandyke!
Ah! there is genius, there is art sublime:
Each tint seems softened by the hand of time,
So true to nature is each scene portrayed!

What wondrous coloring! Ah, such light and shade!
Such gems as those, no modern e'er can equal.
You wouldn't say so, if you knew the sequel;
That those Old Masters, over which you glow,
Were painted only sixty days ago!

At base deception soon your sense recoils;
His choicest liquors are essential oils!
While logwood mingles in the rosy wine
That tastes so like the product of the vine.
His champagne, as a sham, eclipses all —
Sour Jersey cider bottled up last Fall!
Their plated goblets, poised on high, they hold,
To toast the king in wine that's labelled "Old."
The vintage "1790" — Sham declares;
'Tis made of beet juice, and soft rotten pears!
The pastry, jellies, and the savory meats
Are each and all, most arrant, base deceits.
Sand in his sugar, plaster in his bread;
Vermilion colors e'en his pepper red.
His Java coffee — chicory, beans, and pease;
Decocted sloe-leaves are his favorite teas!
His milk is watered, and made thick with chalk,
Or from distillery-stables in New York.
"Mock turtle" is the soup that suits his savor;
His sausages have got a canine flavor!
Lard in his butter is no rank offense;
While wooden nutmegs show a gleam of sense!
But his corned beef you'd never eat, of course;
Unless, you're very partial to salt horse!
His basswood hams, carved from and not on blocks!
They're minnows, surely, in that sardine box!

I'd merely mention, while you seize your hat,
That tender rabbit was a maltese cat!

'Tis plain a king can have whate'er he wishes;
I've only named his most luxurious dishes!
Deceitful thus in actions, taste, and manners,
His cabbage-leaf cigars he calls "Havanas."
His pipe, it is *mere sham* (excuse the pun),
His watch a pinchbeck, never known to run!
His carriage shaky, and got up for show;
His stylish horses foundered long ago!
With *sawdust* bran, and oats from *shoe-pegs* whittled,
The story goes the quadrupeds are victualed!
The books are plagiaries which meet his views;
His steamboat-boilers have defective flues!
From quaker guns I guess there's no report!
The list is lengthy — let us cut it short.

From Humbug Palace and its gilded towers,
Its glare and glitter, its enticing bowers,
The Muse conducts you through the busy land
Where abject millions bow to his command;
And as from Vice she lifts the gorgeous veil,
Your heart shall sicken and your cheek turn pale.
Now don't imagine this is strictly true,
I know you'll laugh before I'm fairly through.
Despite each sad and gloomy phase of vice,
I've not left out what's most essential — spice.
What were a band without their rolling drums?
What were plum-puddings if they had no plums?
What were the bravest soldiers without guns?
Or humorous verse without redeeming puns?

In childhood's days, so innocent and bright,
Flowers bloomed along our path, and silvery light
Fell o'er us from a myriad shining spheres;
Wild, gushing songs were ringing in our ears,
Bewitching fancies dancing through our brain;
Our hearts were joyous and without a stain.
O, innocence of youth, we knew no guile
Nor base deceit that lurks beneath a smile.
Upon the breast of Truth, in fond embrace,
Content we lay our little childish face,
And gazing upward with our pleading eyes
She sang for us her sweetest lullabies.
O, thought revolting to our inmost heart,
Each day we journey all our dreams depart;
Each day we mingle in the busy strife,
Each day we thread the labyrinths of life,
How oft those sinful words our lips repeat, —
"The world's a mockery and our lives a cheat!"
Ah, is our wisdom then — a pearl of price —
Which shows us less of virtue, more of vice?
Like wayward children from the lap of Truth,
Each year we've further strayed, till now, forsooth,
Ripe wisdom says, within a well she's found —
We miss her presence — wonder if she's drowned!

Stray through the world, in fact, search where you will,
King Sham asserts his vast dominion still.
Deceit, alas, we find it everywhere!
'Tis in the food we eat, the clothes we wear;
The toper drinks it in his frequent toddy,
It decks the soldier in his tattered shoddy;
We don it with our hats beyond dispute,

The ladies flaunt it in their silks of jute!
We burn it in the running, wasting taper,
We tread upon 't with soles of wood or paper!
We fly to it to cure us of our ills —
Who does not find it in his monthly bills?
'Tis in religion and in every creed,
While in the papers, 'tis one half we read!

Merchants adulterate their goods and wares,
Mechanics' work is done to need repairs!
The Poet even, and the man of letters,
Oft shine in plumage borrowed from their betters.

Behold the Judge, exemplar of the right;
The difference 'twixt him and yon wretch is slight:
One struck a thoughtless blow, no doubt 'twas cruel;
The judge has "killed his man," in every duel!
If you are poor the sentence must prevail —
Prepare to linger months, or years, in jail.
But if you're rich, consoling is the thought —
The judge and jury are already bought!

The Lawyer's crafty cunning we abhor,
Who picks a pocket as he picks a flaw!
And loads the scales of justice with such skill
They'll turn toward Error, place them as you will!

The Preacher who in language all but tender,
Doth prate of sin, last night was on a bender!
The widows and old maids all praise him highly,
Because he's single and makes love so slyly!

Yon sanctimonious man with downcast eye,

Is but a villain of the deepest dye.
A canting hypocrite, who patters prayers
And apes the saint, to veil his secret snares.
Who talks of Christian grace, and yet would thrust
Poor starving wretches in the very dust;
Sick, suffering, dying, he must have his rent;
They totter forth from crowded tenement.
All this he'd do, and he would never rue it,
Unless he thought some mortal saw him do it!
Throughout the week he talks of Zion's flocks —
On Sunday robs the contribution-box!

The Missionary glibly begs our dimes,
To send the gospel into heathen climes.
Yes, lavish money on the savage sinners,
Our starving poor can go without their dinners!
Do darkened minds no rays of truth require,
Beneath the shadow of the Christian spire?
Let vice and sin run rampant near at hand —
But preach religion in some distant land!

"The People!" is the Politician's cry,
"The People!" shouts he from the rostrum high;
But once elected, and in Congress seated,
How then, by him, are the *dear people* treated?
Before the world each speech the papers quote,
But in the lobby "How much for my vote?"

The Temperance Man has seized a curious whim —
Unless he's sick, no stimulants for him
Which send mankind to ruin double-quick —
Isn't it a pity he's so often sick?
I must alter the metre to level a pun,
And to ask him a question — Why under the sun,

Don't he locate in Tunis, have things his own way,
Where the folks are all under, not *over the Bey?*

The Gambler will relieve you of your "tin,"
To draw you on, will always let you win.
Behold the victim's anxious looking face;
See! he has raised the winning card — the ace.
The ten-spot next — ten-ace-ous silly goose,
Stake your last dollar, then you'll raise the deuce!
Old Pharaoh's host beneath the waters sank,
But Faro's host, more prudent, keep the bank!
Let gamblers "whip the devil 'round the stump,"
For they'll be startled at the final trump!

The Public Speaker gives a sham discourse,
And then expects you'll cheer him till you're hoarse.
His flowery figures are a mere pretense,
He would palm off as sound and sober sense;
While Latin phrases with the prefix "Dog,"
Obscure his meaning like a London fog!
With swaying body, and his arms thrown high,
Away he soars toward Fancy's glowing sky.
Here, in his manuscript, he's left a pause,
To note the place where he expects applause!
If you don't give it, then he's in a fix,
For down he comes, just "like a thousand bricks,"
And seeks in vain to signal with his fist,
The train of thought his drowsy hearers missed!
Such, with a parting shot, I must assail —
He who thus spouts is "very like a whale!"

With painted wounds, the Beggar e'en will try
To claim a pittance from the passers-by.

One sturdy fellow feigns a broken leg;
Though hale in body, strong in limb, doth beg.
Another still as shrewd, all work doth shun,
By stopping strangers with his plaintive dun:
No work — 'tis three days since he tasted meat,
Wants some few cents to save him from the street.
Give him a dime — then mark how straight a line
He makes toward shops with "Liquors" on the
    sign!

A little child was once the tool of those
Who made a living shamming human woes.
She sobbed a tale to suit such exigencies:
Her father dead, no money for expenses.
Yes, in a coffin lying cold and dead,
She had no money, e'en to buy some bread.
If you would go with her (she sobbed again)
You'd find him in a garret, in ——— Lane.
A tale so piteous touched a generous mind;
Who took her hand, and with an impulse kind,
Sought out the drear abode of want and pain;
And, sure enough, there lay a corpse, 'twas plain.
He felt compassion for such bitter sorrow,
Gave from his purse, and said he'd call to-morrow;
Went down the stairs, and gained the narrow lane;
Ah, in his flurry, he'd forgot his cane!
Quick he returned, and softly oped the door,
The sight transfixed him to the spot with awe —
The sight, indeed, was terrible and strange —
There sat the corpse a counting o'er the change!

How many a rich man of our goodly land,
Grasped tight his hoarded gold with clenchèd hand.

In vain distress and want approached his door
To crave a pittance from his countless store;
In vain the poor beseeched, in vain they plead —
But mark the sequel when the man was dead:
His will was opened, and, as there recorded,
Rich institutions got the gold he hoarded.
The papers praised his noble heart and mind,
His generous deeds (that is, the ones he signed)!
His kind consideration for the poor
(He didn't overload their stomachs, sure)!
His splendid charities (when he was dead)!
This, and much more, the smiling skeptic read.
Alive, no man was ever more despised,
He died — how soon a saint was canonized!

Some merchants seem to interest wholly lost,
And always sell their fabrics less than cost!
Though one would think such men extremely rash,
They seem to prosper, and make lots of cash!
Large stocks of goods which others seek to slaughter;
Are only "Slightly Damaged — Wet by Water!"
Could you but look within their stores at night,
You would be startled at the strangest sight:
Fresh goods are taken from the shelves and cases,
Unfolded, tumbled, thrown in various places;
Bedrenched with water, and dragged to and fro
Through dust and dirt, till spots begin to show!
Then piled on counters, — what a grand display
For bargain-seekers on the coming day,
Who wouldn't buy the goods when clean and nice,
But since they're damaged, pay a higher price!

The stuff called Brandy, made upon our soil,

A base admixture with essential oil,
When it to France and back the trip has made,
Is placed in bonded warehouse, duty paid;
Wiseacres who before had stood aloof,
Pronounce it Cognac of the highest proof!
Of pure Champagne, the fact has been exhumed,
France yields one tenth of what is here consumed!
The charm of e'en the best Cigars would vanish,
Without the halo of a lie in Spanish!
Distilling Extracts yearly sold the trade,
Would busy Lubin more than one decade!
The fact unknown, or thoroughly disguised,
Our home productions are well patronized!

A myriad shams, on every hand we see;
Doctors grow rich although they disagree.
While one prescribes a liberal dose for all,
That of another is minutely small.
One showers with water, packs in ice;
Another calls this practice an enormous vice;
One lets you eat whate'er your palate craves;
Unless you nearly starve another raves.
These learned doctors oft consult together
In doubtful cases, as, for instance, whether
There yet remains the shadow of a chance
For one who lays unconscious in a trance —
Whose strange disease quite baffles all the skill
Of those whose motto is to "cure or kill."
In breathless silence they most closely scan
The livid features of the dying man.
The case was clearly hopeless, so they said;
Yet all agreed the sick man must be bled.
But when they plunged a lancet in his arm,

His sense returned, he started in alarm : —
"Where am I? Bless me, what an awful fright!
Why, blast your eyes, old hoss, I'm only tight!"
A nervous man persuades himself he's ill,
Old Bolus gives the man a single pill,
Whose healing virtues, let it here be said,
Were good as wheat, since it was made of bread!
The man revives, a wondrous change we see,
The doctor chuckles at his liberal fee!
Betwixt the doctors, doses large and small,
The wonder is, that we survive at all!

I've dealt quite gently with the wise M.D.'s,
But curse the chaps who never got Degrees;
Or, if they did, they bought them ready-made,
Since making parchments has become a trade!
They advertise such nostrums in the prints
As Hifalutin Balm — sure cure for squints!
If croup bids fair to strangle you or throttle,
Of Bluffum's Balsam try a single bottle;
Just keep a taking till your health returns,
And bear in mind — it's excellent for burns!
If you have pimples, blotches on your face,
Buy Cureall's Salve, which never leaves a trace.
He's got some hundred testimonials, too,
He wrote them all himself, that's very true.
One "salt-rheum cure," convincing in its way,
Increased the sales a hundred gross a day!
If your disease appears to be the chronic,
Why swallow down the Universal Tonic.
If "rheumatis" is tugging at your "jints,"
Try Limber's Lotion — always ask for pints!
Or grasp the wire of some magnetic box,

Which shocks the feelings with electric shocks!
If at the rest you feel somewhat aggrieved,
A cordial should be cordially received!
Gigantic posters, and huge, flaming bills,
Announce the virtues of new-fangled pills.
Quacks make large fortunes through their rapid sale,
This is the Age of Pills — so pill-age must prevail!

For beardless youths a tempting snare they lay —
Luxuriant whiskers and moustaches gay,
Are forced to grow on smoothest lips and cheeks,
Reducing Nature's task to one of weeks!
It cost a dollar for the worthless stuff,
A youth applied it, and — why sure enough,
Intently gazing in the glass, he saw
A splendid crop of blisters on his jaw!
More trifling venture was the postage stamp,
Enclosed by thousands to the graceless scamp,
Who said he'd send a recipe by mail,
Which had been tried and never known to fail,
Producing whiskers and moustaches too;
In just three minutes, which was strictly true.
The long expected letter from New York
This sage direction gave — "Apply burnt cork."

Among the many shams, so very shocking,
I think the shrewdest one is Spirit Knocking.
'Tis plain that spirits knock men in the gutter,
And they are carried homeward on a shutter;
But that the spirits should knock over tables,
Or make them dance the polka, are mere fables.
Yes, they are wise and very knowing chaps,
Who hold mankind enraptured by their raps!

This, I affirm, although a paradox —
John Knox, when preaching, was not preaching knocks!

King Sham exerts his greatest power and sway
O'er all the humbugs of the present day;
What takes so well, or draws with such a force,
As "Codfish Mermaids," or, a "Woolly Horse;"
As "Learned Mice," or "Educated Fleas;"
"Live Whales imported from the Polar Seas,"
"A Living Skeleton," "a Western Giant,"
Or, "Ground and Lofty Tumbling" most defiant.
Outside the circus tent, what side-shows thrive,
Where calves with two legs gaze at one with five!
Great wonders must the public oft behold,
Though ten to one they get most badly sold!
Something to startle, or perchance appall 'em,
As Barnum's "What Is It," or "What d' ye call 'em."

Fair woman! she can never condescend
To base deceit to gain some favorite end.
Alas! 'tis true, as to their forms and faces,
When they're less gifted than the fabled Graces,
They never seem to feel such great restraint
To give their pallid cheeks a coat of paint!
Their forms — yes, friends, the truth must be expressed,
Where Nature fails why cotton does the rest!
Let exercise restore her faded bloom,
And save the languid beauty from the tomb;
Nor give the jovial punster cause to say,
The damsel of the Past's the dam—sel of To-day!

Society's a sham, beyond a doubt,

And few there are but what have found it out.
The crowd of lovely belles and foppish beaux
Who throng gay Fashion's halls — do you suppose
They never practice their alluring arts;
To win our homage or besiege our hearts?
Behold yon fop, quite innocent of brains;
As he fair Julia's fixed attention gains,
What mighty topics they discuss together —
Dumas' last novel, fashion, or the weather!
Enough — for be it fine or be it rainy,
We'll chat awhile with charming Miss Delainy;
Though Beauty, Wealth, and Fashion throng the hall,
The gayest flirt, the ruling star of all!
What sunny smiles to chain our roving gaze;
With pouting lips, ambitious of our praise,
She says she never looked so like a fright —
(We think ourselves she's pretty nearly right!)
But then King Sham's decrees are here obeyed,
So praise her beauty or her rich brocade!
Nor fail to mark, though lavish praise we speak,
'Tis Paris rouge, not blushes, on her cheek!
Not half so much amazed as those who say
They saw a beauty drop her teeth one day!
Nor he whose sweetheart sick three weeks in bed,
Beheld her tresses turn from black to red!

The mistress to the kitchen oft repairs,
And deigns to regulate her house affairs;
While thus engaged, behold the door-bell rings,
Says she: "Quick, Biddy! drop your baking things,
Answer the bell, and mind what you're about,
Be sure and tell the callers that I'm out."
But when she's dressed, and sitting quite at ease,

When ladies call, assiduous strives to please.
The servant enters — "Mrs. Stuckup's card."
Descends and greets her with professed regard.
She says aloud, "I'm glad you've called once more:"
But to herself, "Plague on that horrid bore!"

In all large cities, if you chance to look,
You'll find a class who live "by hook or crook."
The angler's art successfully they've tried,
And hooked their shiners from the human tide!
"Oil," "Gold," or "Silver," was the tempting bait
That lured the gudgeon to his luckless fate.
'Twas in the Keystone State, some years ago,
Petroleum first from wells began to flow
In quantities so vast, some folks astounded,
Began to think the story was *well* founded —
That revolutions of the earth must cease
Because the axis would be drained of grease!
Each great excitement has of course, its limit:
Something will happen that will surely dim it.
So when the thousands rushed in breathless haste,
And bought oil lands, and showed the queerest taste,
Had bored the ground till it was like a strainer, —
It drained their cash, could anything be plainer?
Though wells were struck, a hundred barrels flowing,
The credit side a deficit was showing;
A "quarter" for a barrel — slow at that:
They paid ten hogsheads for the cheapest hat,
Some twenty more, for common "stogy" boots —
Absorbed an aqueduct in Sunday suits!
A fortune large they surely couldn't see,
When reservoirs were emptied on a spree!

And so the "smaller fry" began to mizzle,
With sundry hints that something was a fizzle!

Some years elapsed, petroleum took a rise,
Five Dollars at the Well! met people's eyes.
Excitement reached the very highest pitch,—
The way was open, all might now grow rich;
Invest their cash in one of those affairs,
Consisting of — two hundred thousand shares!
So said each sharper, with a placid smile,
Whose company, of course, had just "struck ile."
"Three thousand barrels — prospect of increasing!"
A flattering tale to those whom they were fleecing;
And based, they said, upon the last reports —
Instead of barrels, it was really quarts!
To place the stock within the people's reach,
The shares were offered at five dollars each!

To get a President had been a sticker;
One night, however, influenced by liquor,
A merchant prince, who joined his name with theirs,
Received a present of ten thousand shares!
Then other gentlemen of wealth and fame
Accepted office when they saw his name.
The public confidence remained unshaken;
In just three weeks, lo, every share was taken!
There came at last a crashing and a breaking,—
Stock they term Oil a great turmoil was making!
Great companies exploded like a rocket;
The holes they bored, alas, were in the pocket!
While those "sardines," who from the shock recoil,
Are not the first whose fate was sealed in oil!

The game was up, Oil Stock was fast declining;
Fresh bait might tempt the gudgeons, so to Mining
Their base of operations they transferred
(Base operations is, perhaps, the word).
Their "oily gammon" of the month before,
Gave place to phrases such as "ore" for "bore;"
"Flowed" changed to "lode," and acres into "feet"—
The transformation was indeed complete.
With "assays" rich (some ass says what will fail!)
Formed companies upon the grandest scale,
Whose "lodes" no miner ever yet could trace,
"Extensions"— which extended into space!
The "yield" unyielding in a truthful test;
For "specimens" from "claims" which paid the best,
And which the owners much preferred to hold,
Were not fair samples of the ones they sold!
Like Mrs. Lot, the lots are often "salted;"
So pray reflect, nor pay a price exalted,
Unless you're certain, when "results" are shown,
The ore the chaps had tested — was their own!

One of those persons who contrive to shirk,
By shrewd devices, anything like work,
Once advertised this very curious myth:
Heirs wanted for the large estate of Smith:
Which lay in England and was still unclaimed.
Five millions sterling was the value named.
All of the name of Smith where'er dispersed,
Perchance might find their fortunes here reversed;
For full particulars concerning same,
Enclose One Dollar to — fictitious name.
The lucky scamp, who this shrewd scheme devised,
Egad! was most amazingly surprised,—

When twenty thousand Smiths, with one accord,
Would-be descendants of some English lord,
Sent him their cash, expecting they would get
A speedy answer — and are waiting yet!

A sweeping censure would my Muse bestow
On those conceited mortals here below,
Who for some action they imagine great,
Present themselves with services of plate!
One does his duty — custom has decreed
A fitting token for so rare a deed!

When War's shrill clarion echoed through the land,
Full fifty thousand claimed some high command;
Had e'en one fifth succeeded, why to-day
Ten thousand Generals would have held their sway.
How strange to hear one hundred Brigadiers
Thunder their orders in — one private's ears!
Despite the legions who our chief assailed,
Thank God! a wiser plan at length prevailed,
Gave birth to what I call a brilliant notion —
The motion *pro* or *con* became *pro*-motion!

Think you in such a time of startling danger,
Sham was forgetful of the public manger?
If you think thus, it is a sorry blunder,
For he got every contract spite of thunder!
Go ask the soldier and he'll tell you so,
Whose wooden soles are gaping at the toe:
His tattered shoddy, should he chance to scan,
Or breeches on the ventilation plan!
He'd emphasize his answer with a "damn,"
And say 'twas furnished by that rascal Sham

The glaring frauds, the brazen-faced deceit,
Are known to all, 'tis useless to repeat.
When brave hearts battled for their country's cause,
To crush rebellion and sustain the laws,
Sham's minions most intensely loyal grew,
And cheered and shouted for the "Boys in Blue;"
When they had fired the Nation's frenzied feeling —
Accomplished wonders — in the way of stealing!
Curse, curse the wretch, who, from low groveling greed,
Would rob his country in her hour of need!
By schemes nefarious, and by tricks expert,
Her substance squander and her means pervert;
Defraud her soldiers in the food they eat,
Clothe them in garments rotten with deceit!
Those high in office at the frauds would wink,
Nor share the blame, although they shared the chink!
Words are in vain — give Justice ample scope:
They've stretched our patience, let them stretch a rope!

Such are the scenes within King Sham's domain
The Muse presents to you in colors plain.
What were the world beneath his bogus sway
But loathsome mockery each night and day.
We'd gaze but to encounter some new cheat,
While gilded traps would spring beneath our feet.
We'd breathe an atmosphere corrupt with vice,
Horrors would freeze our very blood to ice.
There'd be no love, there'd be no smiling faces,
For frowning hate would soon usurp their places;
Earth be transformed to hell, and life a curse,
If Sham, not Truth, controlled the universe.

From Sham's domain thy recreant steps retrace,
Tear off the base insignia of the place ;
Unmask thy visage, spurn each dazzling lie,
And sick of mockery, from its presence fly.
The Priestess Truth, all radiant and divine,
Bids thee approach her pure, unsullied shrine;
Since thou hast learned the folly of deceit,
Thy youthful vows let riper age repeat.
In earth's broad lists, where struggling hosts contend
Be thou Truth's champion, and her cause defend ;
And when Sham's minions seek to bear thee down,
Strive for the victor's wreath or martyr's crown.

THE SEVENTH SON OF A SEVENTH SON.

THE famous Baron Gullemall,
   The prophet and the seer,
Ensconced within an easy chair
   Was feeling rather queer,
And ever and anon he quaffed
   A glass of lager beer.

You'd take him for an aged man;
   His head was white with snows,
Of fourscore winters, one would think,
   Did I not here disclose
The secret that he wore a wig,
   And chalked his jolly nose!

While o'er the musty books and charts
   The tapers dimly shine,
A globe celestial and a skull
   Are marshalled into line,
By shapes that bear no semblance to
   Things human or divine!

You see a picture on the wall —
   St. George who slew the dragon;
He looks as if he swallowed down
   The contents of his flagon,

Before he did the mighty deed,
   The Britons love to brag on.

A flaming "Card" in public prints
   Proclaims his wondrous skill,
For by the stars he reads your fate,
   Your fortune good or ill,
And what will surely come to pass —
   When water runs up hill!

This Seventh Son of a Seventh Son
   Whose fame is known abroad,
Whose mystic skill is highly praised
   By noble, duke, and lord —
Forgot, when leaving foreign parts,
   To pay his monthly board!

Of course it was occasioned by
   His haste to reach the ship.
How strange such slips of memory are?
   If in this case you'll dip,
You'll find he kept his memory —
   And gave his friends the slip!

As he was sitting all alone,
   And chuckling o'er his gains;
That craving for the marvelous
   Which haunts poor feeble brains,
Had brought another visitor
   Into his strange domains.

Lo! she who stood before him now,
   Among old maids was classed;

As if to test his wondrous power
　　She questioned of the past;
And towards the Baron's piercing eyes
　　A timid glance she cast.

"You're married, so the stars proclaim —
　　What's this that I descry?
Four children have your union blest —"
　　The maiden gave a sigh,
Then springing to her feet she shrieked —
　　"You cruel monster — fie!"

A well-dressed chap next ventured in,
　　And told him his desire;
"You'll make some noise in the world, my friend,
　　Or every star's a liar."
The Baron's words were verified,
　　For he became town-crier!

A body-snatcher came to see
　　If what folks said was true;
Then says the Baron carelessly —
　　"*Grave subjects* you pursue."
Afraid to have his thoughts laid bare,
　　The man in haste withdrew.

Next, one whose curiosity
　　Had reached the highest pitch,
Desired to see his future wife,
　　And learn if she were rich;
And if her face were beautiful,
　　Or ugly as a witch.

The Baron waved his hand, and lo!
  A panel moved aside,
And dimly through a veil of gauze
  A visage he descried;
He started back as pale as death,
  Intensely horrified.

A fearful oath he would have sworn,
  But he could only groan;
To steal a march on destiny
  He vowed he'd live alone; —
He never spoke to woman more:
  The secret was his own!

Day after day the people came
  To have their fortunes told:
The rich and poor, the young and fair,
  The wrinkled and the old;
While Gullemall, in one short year,
  Ten thousand noodles sold!

Had I the gift of Gullemall,
  Fate's mysteries to explore,
In all the lotteries I'd invest,
  The highest prizes draw!
The hidden wealth of Captain Kidd
  Should see the light once more.

RESPONSE TO A TOAST.

JUST so! I, when invited, raised no doubts
   But what you'd put me through "a *course* of
     sprouts:"
When you ask me to speak, just mind your eye:
A *leaf*, to rustle, must be mighty dry!
Well! on the feast just ended, I'll rehearse
A sort of dish-ertation done in verse;
But this I'll say, lest some should think it strange,
Our range of thought is not the cooking range!
Look at those saucers — say! what sorcery is nigh?
And all those plates, just contemplate and sigh,
To think no more good things you can partake —
You've grown too full (you'll groan e'er morning
     break)!
Shall I emerge from this *grub* state, and fly
With spangled wings through Fancy's glowing sky?
Ah no! my friends, I'll linger with the rest:
To make the laugh go round I'll do my best.
Now hold your sides, for Mirth shall rule the day;
Then light your rocket-jokes, and blaze away!

OYSTERS, FRIED IN CRUMBS.

GIVE Frenchmen frogs, Italians macaroni,
   The cannibal some human thumbs;
The wise *savants*, a well-conditioned pony—
   But give, O, give me "Fried in Crumbs."

In praise of cats and rats the Chinese shout,
   John Bull, to his roast beef succumbs;
Give Hans, the Dutchman, beer and sauerkraut—
   But give, O, give me "Fried in Crumbs."

No doubt the Esquimau, with seal and blubber,
   Is quite content when cold benumbs;
I'd sooner think of chewing India rubber—
   Then give, O, give me "Fried in Crumbs."

I know that salmon and green pease are fine,
   Roast ducks and geese are nice and juicy,
Folks have their likes and dish-likes: I have mine—
   So "Fried in Crumbs"—dear Al. and Lucy.

ON YOUTHFUL LINGUISTS.

AN EPIGRAM.

IN modern schools, the scholars sage,
  When they are sixteen years of age,
Profess to know, yet never *speak*,
The French, the Latin, and the Greek.
These prodigies, when fully grown,
Speak every tongue — except their own!

VERSES AND REVERSES.

THE ferry-boat approached the shore,
  A cat, seen by the skippers,
Began to pur around the slip —
  Yet not around the slip-pers!

Behold the type of innocence
  That skips across the green;
You know full well a lamb is meant —
  Yet no lam-(m)ent, I ween!

O, he was such a jolly chap,
  The owner of the hall;
He was not one who bawls aloud —
  Yet he allowed the ball!

A roofer once was sorely pressed,
  When bills came pouring in;
For though the chap could tin the plank —
  He couldn't "plank the tin!"

A gambler at the point of death,
  This sober moral shows:
However well he throws the die —
  He dies with awful throes!

A chimney-sweep, his insults base,
  On Biddy 'gan to heap;
When she who used to sweep the floor —
  Turned round to floor the sweep!

A quack once saw a vision rise,
  Which fairly took away sense:
Not "Patience on a Monument" —
  But monuments o'er patients!

We gaze upon the world, and shout:
  "Will wonders never cease?"
We seize a pig and grease its tail —
  Yet see no Tale of Greece!

A man may dote upon his aunt,
  Yet not on anti-dotes!
A blacksmith often notes a forge —
  Who never forges notes!

Don't fly into a passion, friend,
  And raise a furious rumpus;
You placed the compass in a box —
  You did not "box the compass!"

A man may sail across the deep —
  And not be "half seas over!"
Pearl divers get in awful straits —
  But not the Straits of Dover!

From filly madly dashing by,
  A quickly sprang aside;

That 'twas a-filly-A-shun — no
　Logician would decide.

Like Walton, angle in the brook,
　Not like a pack of ninnies —
And what you there descry, may be
　A fin — yet not a Fin-is!

NED BROWN; OR, THE BITER BIT.

A PARAPHRASE.

SEE Scituate, that famous town,
   'Tis situated near the sea!
Where lived Joe Kerr, of great renown,
   A great jo-ker was he!

Once, when his house was furnished new,
   With everything that's grand and fine,
He thought he'd ask the favored few
   To see the change — and dine.

Now, on the morning of that day,
   Ned Brown, who was a "knowing bird,"
As he was passing by that way
   Called in to say a word.

As Joe was shaving at the glass,
   He told friend Brown to look at all
The changes he had made, then pass
   Into his dining hall.

While there, friend Brown, who oft had tried
   To get the start of him in jokes,
For once was certain he espied
   Good luck on Fortune's spokes.

Then slyly from his pocket drew
   A small tape-measure, took the height
Of splendid tables which he knew
   Would be in use that night.

He told his friend he could not stay,
   And gave some very trivial reason;
Says Joe, "Good-bye! to-night, I pray,
   Be sure and come in season."

The guests arrive, each takes his seat,
   Course after course their palates try;
In shortest metre eat the meat,
   And pass the parsnips by.

One quails before a tempting quail,
   And says that they are merely shams;
One ailing chap declines the ale,
   Yet clamorous calls for clams.

This broth the "broth o' a b'y" would please,
   Some witty one at length declares;
While pease his appetite appease,
   Despairing of the pears.

The host conniving, soon their knives
   They bury deep in berry pies;
Impeach him who for peaches strives
   To get the largest size.

The cloth removed, impatient Ned
   Declared the tables were quite fine;
The carving was so rich, he said,
   Of such a neat design.

The nick of time! — so in he chimed,
    As thick their praises round him fly:
"There's only just one fault I find,
    They are a trifle high."

"Too high?" the host replies, "too high?
    I think they surely are too low."
"A great mistake," says Ned; "my eye
    Is quite correct, I know,

"And two-feet-six should always be
    The height of tables such as these;
They're higher by an inch, I'm free
    To bet you what you please."

"Were I not owner, by the zounds!
    And certain of the height, I swear
I'd bet you, Ned, full fifty pounds,
    To see the thing proved fair."

"I'm *certain* too, the height I know,
    My eye, I say, is always true;
I'll bet the money with you, Joe,
    Now hold the stakes, friend Drew."

"'Tis done; come servant, bring the yard" —
    "Hold! Joe, now don't be quite so swift;
For once, my boy, — don't take it hard, —
    I've set you all adrift.

"For when I called this very morn,
    I took the height, and set it down;
Was I not certain? own the corn,
    And pass along each crown."

What peals of laughter follow now,
   While in the midst Joe's voice is heard: —
"One moment, friends, if you'll allow,
   I'd like to say a word.

"You were quite right;" a glance he cast,
   But what it meant, no one suspected;
"One thing, I know, whatever passed,
   The mirror true reflected.

"I saw the whole, and well I guessed
   What witty thought had seized your brain,
And noticed, as your hand I pressed,
   The smile you would restrain.

"You left — don't look so pale, I beg;
   At jokes, you know, you should not flinch:
I seized a saw, and from each leg
   I cut off — just an inch!"

"How 'bout that eye?" "I own up now,"
   'Mid roars of laughter muttered Brown;
"And here's the stakes, well won, I vow —
   Don't tell it to the town."

They left quite late, with a jovial song,
   A whispered joke, a sharp retort;
You think the legend is too long —
   The leg-end was too short!

THE OFFICE SEEKER.

ELECTION day is near at hand,
    The "Cards" will soon appear
Announcing that friend Jones will stand
    For office — and the beer.

And though he oft hath passed you by,
    Amid the bustling crowd,
He soon will say, — "How are you, Cy?
    My boy you do me proud."

To be polite to all, he strives;
    His voice could not be milder,
As he inquires about their wives
    And all the little "childer."

He holds your hand within his own,
    And glibly chats awhile;
Then says, in such a winning tone, —
    "Let's take a friendly smile."

Says — while a steaming "Tom and Jerry"
    Is gliding down your throat, —
"I was adverse to running — very,
    But how about your vote?"

The full returns the papers quote,
    And Jones looks most forlorn;
He gave a "horn" to get a vote —
    He got it — in a horn!

THE SPREADING RUMOR.

TWO antiquated spinsters sat
   Commenting on the news;
With copious draughts of Hyson tea
   To clarify their views.

Says Gossip One to Gossip Two:
   "While shopping in the town,
Old Mrs. Pry to me remarked —
   Smith *bought* his goods of Brown."

Says Gossip Two to Gossip Three,
   Who cast her eyelids down:
"I've heard it said, to-day, my friend,
   Smith *got* his goods from Brown."

Says Gossip Three to Gossip Four,
   With something of a frown:
"I've heard strange news — what do you think:
   Smith *took* his goods from Brown!"

Says Gossip Four to Gossip Five,
   Who blazed it round the town:
"I've heard, to-day, such shocking news —
   Smith *stole* his goods from Brown!"

BACHELOR BABBITT.

A PATHETIC NARRATIVE.

A BACHELOR gay was dressing for the ball,
A handsome fellow, well proportioned, tall.
He was in that queer state (don't blush, Miss Prude)
That common parlance would determine, nude;
That's not the word — *en dishabille* I'd say;
Thread, needles, buttons, all around him lay.
Inspects his linen, wherefore? you may ask,
But bachelors, friends, know all about the task.
It seemed quite plain, that long-continued habit,
Caused this procedure on the part of Babbitt.
Back he recoiled, as if a rattlesnake
Had stung him thrice; his very limbs did quake,
His cheek grew ghastly, while his eyes were fixed
As though the thing was looking rather mixed!
He staggered — fell — as if from mortal hurt,
Exclaiming: "Heavens! a button on my shirt!"
Senseless he fell, his head against a table,
The fall alarmed the lodgers ('tis no fable);
They forced his door, upon the upper story,
And there they found him lying pale and gory.
They raised him up, and placed him on the bed,
And when his senses came (some hours, 'tis said),
He wildly stared at each familiar face —
They asked the cause, he made a strange grimace.

"Saw you a ghost, a goblin, or a flirt?"
"A sight more strange — *a button on my shirt!*"

MORAL.

O laundress! from this tale a lesson learn,
Remove all buttons ere you dare return
Our "wash"; for sewing buttons is our habit,
And we might share the dreadful fate of Babbitt.

SOLD!

ALONG Broadway two dandies slowly passed,
And quizzing glances at the ladies cast.
Soon they beheld a form they thought divine,
With Paris hat and swelling crinoline,
Tripping along before them on the pave.
"Jove! she's enough to make a fellow rave,"
Said Charles Augustus with a mincing smile,
"Let's pass ahead, my boy, and see her style."
"Agreed!" says Ned, and onward quick they budge;
In passing, Ned gave Charley's ribs a nudge,
And both looked back at her they thought so gay —
Their faces showed a look of blank dismay!
Despite the Paris hat, gay flounce, and frill,
She proved — a negro wench, "dressed out to kill!"

A LOGICAL CONCLUSION.

THOU'RT like a treasury note, sweet Annie Lee,
    Grant me thy hand, and I will prove it thee.
Hark ye! then say that I'm your sworn defender —
  A tender Lee gal is, a le-gal tender!

SCANDAL AND TEA.

I'M aware that the grounds in our coffee, my friend,
    Furnish very good grounds for complaint;
Although scandal and tea, wise philosophers blend,
  One is easier to *draw* than to paint!

I have found that *hot water* to each is allied,
  (Grave discussion, now pray don't begin it!)
For you cannot have one without it's applied,
  Nor the other, unless you are in it!

PIKE'S PEAKERS OF '59.

A HUMOROUS HISTORY OF THE PIKE'S PEAK EXCITEMENT.

RUSHING wildly to and fro,
   Everybody on the go,
Rumors never travel slow,
   While the golden ones go kiting!
And excited thousands seek,
Fortunes large in Cherry Creek,
In the region of Pike's Peak,
   Where big nuggets lie inviting.

In each town and in each village,
No more thought of land or tillage;
All seem given up to pillage —
   No one ever saw the like.
"Posey county"[1] is in motion,
All "South Bend" has seized the notion,
"Prairie schooners,"[2] ne'er on ocean,
   Leave the classic shores of Pike!

River towns are full of folks,
Cattle, — yea, a thousand yokes
Hitched unto the wagon spokes, —
   Stubborn mules, and horses frisky!

Flour and bacon, picks and crows,
Frying-pans and — what are those?
Barrels of — the devil knows!
  But I think they call it whiskey!

Now you trip upon a rope,
Fall between a box of soap
And a keg of lard; I hope
  That no bones were broke in falling.
Folks will laugh at such a sight,
And one fellow swears you're tight,
And of course there is a fight
  And somebody gets a mauling!

Such a noise — ox-whips a cracking,
Trains a starting, men a packing,
Dust a rising, horses backing —
  Second Babel on the earth!
Tongues confused and wagons shattered,
And again mankind are scattered!
Slightly bruised and mud-bespattered —
  What a carnival of mirth!

Camping out upon the plains,
Thinking of the golden gains
That will pay you for your pains,
  And the comforts you have missed.
Your first biscuits — ar'n't they splendid?
Saleratus richly blended;
Grease and talent both expended —
  Frying bacon to a crisp!

Standing guard at dead of night,
Indians have been seen in sight,

And you tremble with affright,
  Thinking of those scalps all gory!
How you shot your leading mule,
That was grazing near a pool,
Roused the camp, who called you — fool!
  And would'nt listen to your story.

Miles of wagon-tops in sight,
Stretching o'er the plains, so white,
When the sun was shining bright,
  In those days of "Fifty-nine."
Some were trudging with a pack
Bound upon their aching back,
Some drew handcarts o'er the track,
  Towards their Mecca's golden shrine.

One had loaded down an ox
With his tools, provision box;
And he thought it "knocked the socks"
  Off of any other "feller."
When his strength began to fail,
Then he grasped the "critter's" tail,
And kept jogging on the trail,
  With his famous ox-propeller!

Outfits strange and very queer,
Every style of running gear,
Some so odd it seems quite clear
  That old Noah first gave the order.
While McGrew, the story ran,
Pushed wheelbarrow like a man:
Such was his house-keeping plan;
  Spite of that — he took a boarder!

See the sides of wagons traced
With inscriptions — all but chaste ;
Some are witty, some in taste,
   Let us pause awhile and ponder :
There 's " Pike's Peak or Bust ! " — sure they
Are true grit and bound to stay ;
Three months later, plain as day,
   We may read they're — " Bust, by Thunder ! "

" Ho ! for Pike's Peak ! " so they go,
A rough row they'll have to hoe !
And I guess they'll find it so,
   Or I'm mightily mistaken.
There's another going by,
What is that ? — " Root Hog or Die ! "
Looks like pluck ; no doubt they'll try
   Deuced hard to save their bacon.

Those old oxen, so demurely
Do they drag that wagon, surely —
I don't wish to speak obscurely,
   But a snail could give them odds.
And a laugh we can't suppress
As we read, " Lightning Express ; "
There is wit and nothing less ;
   What a joker, by the gods !

Here again we're led astray ;
'Tis no joke, the numskulls say ;
And explain it as they may,
   It still more the joke is heightening :
For we learn the words relate
Not to speed, but to the fate

Of their friend and fellow mate,
   And whose death was caused by lightning!

Strike the butt across your leaders;
Now we meet the first stampeders;
Listen to these sorry pleaders,
   What a tale they can unfold!
"Stop! for mercy's sake don't go;
It's all humbug and all blow;
Not a "color"[3] could they show,
   Not a thimbleful of gold."

"Denver is in ashes laid,
And a lively time they made
Hanging settlers, who essayed
   Of their mines a word to speak."
What! are hundreds turning back,
Listening to this silly clack?
Never mind, keep in the track,
   Let the cowards homeward sneak.

Faded are their golden dreams,
For we meet a thousand teams,
All are going back, it seems,
   Swearing — well, words can't express it.
Who can stem this human tide,
That with taunts and jeers deride,
Threaten life and limb beside?
   Very few, I must confess it.

Yet those few were brave and bold,
All along the Platte they strolled,
And at length Pike's Peak behold,
   Spite of hardships without number.

But those eyes on Smoky Hill,
Famine-stricken, never will;
And at night when all is still,
    Stars look down where heroes slumber.

Talk of Progress in her car,
And of Empire with its star
Softly gleaming from afar —
    It is but a poet's flight.
Pioneers — yes, men like they,
Bone and sinew, clear the way,
And when things are all O. K.
    Madame Progress heaves in sight!

Towards Denver City let us now propel,
Of its strange sights and startling wonders tell.
How each log-cabin with dirt-covered roof,
In rainy weather was quite water-proof.
But when no longer storms about them lower,
For days the inmates had their little shower!
Crowds thronged the gambling halls by day and night;
How they did scatter in a row or fight!
At Denver Hall, moved by an impulse strong,
One frightened pilgrim took the sash along!
But dog-fights were too good a thing to lose,
Nineteen a day just met the people's views;
That is, if each his mind had freely spoken,
For dull monotony and heads were broken!
Before a dog-fight lasted half a minute,
No use of talking, all the men were in it!
Mankind at dances 'reft of woman's charms,
Tied handkerchiefs about each other's arms.

The "knot was tied" which changed some men to women!
They blushed and gushed — the dances went on swimmin'!

With canvas tents how white the town-site grew;
From morn till night long trains were passing through
The crowded streets; strange groups were gathered there,
At which each pilgrim looks with vacant stare.
Mankind for once in roughest garb he sees
Move helter-skelter like a swarm of bees!
And there was one strange object of conjecture,
He might be called a spectre or prospecter;
Because they're both so very near akin,
Where one leaves off the other must begin!
Long bushy hair upon his shoulders lay,
His grizzly beard unshorn for many a day;
His eyes were piercing and his features grim;
His hat was crownless and without a rim,
From which the tail of luckless fox doth droop,
The only ornament to which he'd stoop.
Within his belt an old six-shooter thrust,
Not thrice, six times he's armed, whose quarrel's — dust!
He is a type of this adventurous class;
A few more comments and we'll let them pass.
Old flannel shirts they wore, with many a patch,
While "graybacks"[4] brought the wearers to the scratch!
Oft were their breeches with old flour-sacks mended,
In which more truth than poetry was blended;
For by the brand upon his trousers' seat,

There goes a chap, "Made from Selected Wheat!"
We cannot help exclaim, why in the deuce
Was that small man "Put up for Family Use?"
And why that ponderous chap we lately met
Was falsely branded "Ninety-eight Pounds Net?"
To those rough men, a tribute would I pay,
Who "made the riffle"[5] in that early day;
Who set to work, though adverse tales were told,
And turned the scales with glittering scales of gold!

The Desperado was a savage "cuss,"
Eager to breed a row or raise a muss;
Who snuffed afar the symptoms of a fight,
And drew his "navy" or his "bowie" bright,
And always made it his exclusive "biz"
To mingle in a crowd and "let 'er whiz!"
To shoot at random was a "heap" of fun,
Rare sport to see the people break and run!
His vaunted prowess had such ample swing,
"A man for breakfast"[6] was a common thing.
On him at last the tables swift were turned;
A wholesome lesson, to his cost, he learned.
The "Vigys"[7] pointed to an empty saddle,
And gave him just ten minutes to skedaddle!
But if he "killed his man," why then you see,
Escape was certain, that is — up a tree!

Once early settlers issued forth a call,
A crowd assembled in old Denver Hall,
And after several of the leading speakers
Had touched on subjects pleasing to Pike's Peakers,
One would-be speaker, by the usual game,
Obtained the floor to urge his way to fame.

"George Washington" — in rolling tones he said.
(Applause, which shook the rafters overhead.)
"*George Washington!*" again the words he utters.
(Immense applause, which jarred the window-shutters.)
"GEORGE WASHINGTON!" this time a little higher.
(Renewed applause, — why don't they "holler fire?")
"GEORGE WASHINGTON!" he yelled, in tones
    of thunder.
(Applause grew frightful, and he stood from under.
For those old settlers in that early day,
Thought, doubtless, 'twas the best thing he could say!)
I've heard dull speakers, would to heaven they could
Have uttered anything one half as good.

I asked, one day, a question strictly proper,
About our miles — you may not care a copper!
But then, I thought I'd like to learn the truth,
Some are so long, and some so short, forsooth.
Old Buckskin heard the "quiz" I had propounded,
Took a fresh quid (a quidnunc I had sounded),
"Wal! stranger, reckon I ken make it clear,
I'll tell yer how it is, 'twont seem at all queer;
Fact is, it's plain as pyrites from gravel;
We used to grub the men, tell 'em to travel
Till it gin out, and then (stranger, don't smile),
To kind o' calculate they'd gone ten mile.
Yer see, they'd start; now, some were frugal eaters,
Who never cared a cuss for rain or skeeters;
They pegged ahead, put in the licks quite strong,
And so their miles may be a *leetle* long.
The other chaps, a hungry-gutted set,
Soon lagged behind, with appetites beset,
Ate their allowance, and then shot a buck;

Their miles were short, yer bet your muckie-muck![8]
That's truth outright, that's how we reckon miles,
Or close my peepers up with rat-tail files!"
The tale may please those who love fun and mirth;
I give Old Buckskin's word for what it's worth.
Not much, perhaps, the hearer doubtless thinks;
I asked, and found — it wasn't worth two drinks.

We owe our gratitude to Horace Greeley,
Who shed for us his printer's ink so freely;
In Denver Hall when Horace "spoke his piece,"
For once, all gambling operations cease.
A "three card monte" chap forsook his game,
Politely loaned his table — Horace took the same.
On agriculture and our great resources,
He marshalled all his intellectual forces;
Some hundreds heard him, and when he was through,
The chap resumed his game, and he withdrew.
His ears were greeted, ere he reached the door,
With words whose like he never heard before:
"Come down! Come down! roll up here one and all;
Ready to size your pile! bets large or small!
Who turns the card? who wins the dollars shining?
No *agriculture here!* this game's like mining!"

Among the many thousands who came here,
To make their fortunes in a single year,
Was Stubbs — six-footer, with an awkward manner,
Who hailed, 'twas said, from Squashtown, Indiana.
Upon the plains he dreamt about a nugget
So big, it took just fourteen men to lug it;
And waking, strove the treasure vast to seize,
But found it was the moon behind the trees.

Stubbs sought the Gregory mines. Says he, "The deuce!
These miners call a water-trough a sluice;
Accordin' to the gineral talk and clamor,
I thought they chipped the chunks off with a hammer."
He worked *one day*, began to have the dumps,
And threw the dust aside, in search for lumps.
Folks cursed the region, and he took th' alarm,
Thought he'd go back and settle on a farm!
So back he goes; once more upon the plains,
Folks crowd around him, ask about his gains;
He told them all, that he and his friend Usher,
Were going to the States *to get a Crusher!*"

    There is a legend weird and strange,
        About a golden peak;
    And where it rose, or in what range,
        I cannot fully speak.
    But this I know, in "Fifty-nine"
        The story oft was told,
    How early settlers used to mine
        This solid mass of gold.

    They built a mighty curious craft,
        It rather kind o' got 'em;
    'Twas fashioned something like a raft,
        With iron rasps on bottom.
    'Twas hoisted to the mountain top,
        A chap got on to steer it,
    And then they kind o' let 'er drop,
        Or something very near it.

Away it went like all possessed,
  Folks had to stand from under,
For ten miles round, the miners guessed
  It was a clap of thunder!
O! it made such a frightful din
  They wished they had not loosed it;
Not all the graters made of tin,
  Together had produced it.

The chap who rode this strange machine,
  Thought nothing sure could knock it.
(A charge of nitro-glycerine
  I guess would slightly rock it;
But then this was before the world
  Had learned to fear the "critter.")
The golden shavings round him curled,
  And covered him with litter.

He glanced behind, and then gave one
  Unearthly shriek of laughter,
For golden shavings by the ton
  Were swiftly following after.
And yet this chap was not afraid,
  He wore a placid smile;
He went ahead of what he made,
  And yet he made his pile!

THE TURKEY WAR.

A TALE OF TURKEYS — NOT A TURKISH TALE.

A CLEAN RECORD OF A FOWL AFFAIR.

*Served up with such a variety of spicy ingredients that no
"stuffing" was deemed necessary.*

INVO-CA-SHUN.

The Muse is meant when on the Nine we dwell;
There is a-muse-ment in *nine*-pins as well,
Or any other nine you choose to mention,
Especially a femi-*nine* convention!
The cat o' *nine* tails is a perfect whaler:
Attest, the back of an unruly sailor!
Nine tails with but a single cat,
Nine tails that *beat* as one!
Against the ca*nine* since objections weigh,
Descend ye Nine, the Nine without the ca!
An invo-ca-shun without more ado,
As good's the average, and about as true.

"The Turkey War! the expression's lame,
I don't dispute the fowls are *game*,
But give your theme more fitting name,
And say at once — The War in Turkey!"
'Tis not the Turks I'm poetizing,
That you mistake is not surprising;

THE TURKEY WAR.

The (Y) East's mixed up with many a rising!
   Though powder's harmless when from Durkee!

You shouldn't show so much conceit;
The Turkey War, I here repeat,
Although it shows no brilliant feat,
   No subtle stratagem discloses,
Was quite a marvel in its way:
A speck of war, a bloodless fray,
Sweet-scented muss — old settlers say —
   Although it was no War of Roses.

A load of turkeys, think of that!
In splendid order, nice and fat;
To Denver came, not up the Platte,
   The usual route supplies were brought,
But from the settlements below,
The Arkansas or Huerfano.[9]
Perchance the latter (guess that's so!)
   Because they caused a *war for naught!*

Indeed it was a luscious cargo,
On which the "bummers"[10] laid embargo,
And such a one as ne'er Wells, Fargo—
   Within their "caravans"[11] have stowed.
While those who gazed with longing eyes,
Were filled with wonder and surprise,
And some with turkeys, I surmise,
   Who had no claim upon the load!

The owner was beguiled away,
By fellows who seemed mighty gay,
And round the city he did stray,

A seeing sights and drinking cobblers.
When to his wagon he returned,
Exclaiming as his loss he learned —
"Was it for this 'freeze out' I spurned,
    To lose by *roast-in'* all my gobblers?"

A species of another kind
Of gobbler than he left behind,
More *taking in their ways*, you'll find,
    Had taken off all they could lug;
The meeting seemed to each beholder,
Like that of Greeks, though centuries older,
Since one's *best hold* was, from the shoulder!
    Of course 'twas followed by a *tug!*

In Denver as in Denmark, there
Was something rotten, folks declare;
To put the matter fair and square,
    The thieves had got a Den in each!
No use to try to save your bacon;
If left within their reach — 'twas taken!
E'en *terra firma* might awaken
    Some keen regrets — if out of reach!

No hanging out of clothes to dry,
For fear some rascal prowling nigh;
Might take occasion on the sly,
    To make a raid along the line!
Upon retiring, it is said,
Men placed their boots beneath their head,
And wore their clothes through wholesome dread
    They'd take each stitch — and ne'er save nine!

So when the people heard the tale,
They vowed at once they would assail
The *turkey gobblers* without fail;
   The human bipeds, not the feathered!
To spit their vengeance on that class
Who were already spitted, were a farce!
To make *no bones* of those, alas!
   Whose flesh had been already gathered!

Proceedings were at once devised,
Of which the rascals were apprised.
Although they were somewhat surprised
   At what they termed the best of jokes,
They swore they'd fight it out, by thunder!
At their abuse I cannot wonder;
Since *turkey* they had rent asunder,
   They'd naught to fear *in-sultan* folks.

Perchance those who the mischief planned
Ate half-cleaned gizzards, and the band
Determined thus to make a stand
   Whilst they were feeling full of grit!
So, in the face of quiet folk
A loaded pistol they would poke;
A very pleasant sort of joke,
   Though rather *pointed*, I admit.

Parading through the crowded street,
Denouncing those they chanced to meet,
Their list of crimes had been complete,
   Had they not missed their murderous aim!
They swore revenge, and made a threat
To burn the town of Denver yet,

Before another sun should set —
  Which would have been a burning shame!

Though cackling geese saved ancient Rome,
According to historic tome,
If "sound upon the *goose*," their home
  Was doubly threatened with a crash.
What if they were consigned to fame,
Through circumstances much the same,
And coming ages should exclaim —
  " 'Twas Turkeys settled Denver's hash!"

Forth came the brave, undaunted Rangers,
To calm the fears of timid strangers;
To guard the town from threatened dangers,
  Until the rising of the sun.
As into patrols they divided,
Disturbances at once subsided:
To run no risk, the rogues decided;
  Of course there was no risk — to run.

Next day the citizens agreed,
Three perpetrators of the deed
Must leave the town; by taking heed,
  A *throat affection's* stopped in time.
From trick to trick, through Fate's decree,
The Climb-Act's reached at last, you see,
When they must either "climb a tree,"
  Or seek a more congenial clime!

The rogues obeyed the people's fiat,
The town resumed its wonted quiet,
But still we suffer from that riot
  Which years ago the settlers quelled.

The turkeys scarce, and awful dear,
By *twos* and *threes* arriving here;
Because somehow the farmers fear,
   A load *at once* — would be corraled.

There's nothing in the *sobriquet*,
By which we designate th' affray,
To keep you farming chaps away;
   Then let your idle fancies cease.
Bring on your turkeys, I insist:
Temptation's great, but we'll resist;
A Turkey War can ne'er exist,
   When *all* are anxious for a *piece*.

SHOVELS AND PICKS; OR, THE MODEL SUPERINTENDENT.

TO Colorado once there came
   A handsome young New Yorker,
Charles Noble Codfish (scaly name),
   Dundreary style of talker;
Got up "regardless of expense,"
   His head a mass of curls;
With just that lack of common sense
   So pleasing to the girls.

To superintend a mine he came:
   His Company was rich,
And honored drafts that bore his name,
   Without the slightest hitch.
Yet not one fact the fellow knew
   About the mining region.
Guess those of which the same is true
   Would number quite a legion.

His mining dialect, behold,
   How sadly 'twas neglected;
With "lodes" of cabbages or gold
   His "shafts" were all connected.
He'd heard of "range" — the cooking kind;
   Thought "ores" to boats applied;

While "vein" was something to his mind
   Indicative of pride.

He had a duty to fulfill,
   And so he set about it:
He built a most expensive mill —
   How could they do without it?
When everything was *a la mode*,
   He made a trial run;
The ore was from their richest lode,
   There must have been a ton.

Fire up, fire up! the whistle blows;
   The clattering wheels revolve;
Thump, thump! thump, thump! such stamps as those
   The mystery soon will solve.
A strange result doth he behold,
   With courage let him brave it;
For though the ore were two thirds gold,
   That mill could never save it.

He went upon the biggest sprees,
   And in the lowest hovels;
Disbursements made at times like these,
   Were classified as "shovels!"
Such transformations he produced,
   By certain clever tricks,
That pick-adilloes were reduced
   Till they were only "picks."

The festive youths of Central City
   Declared he was a "cuss;"

Cards, billiards, liquor — what a pity
   To squander money thus.
The way in which the chap evades
   His losses, beats the dickens!
While "shovels" shield unlucky "spades,"
   The "picks" protect the "pickings."

He sent his statements to the East
   In most elaborate shape;
A quire of foolscap at the least,
   With eyelets and red tape.
The writing was like copper-plate,
   With no unseemly blot;
The *t's* were crossed as sure as fate,
   The *i's* had each a dot.

The smallest item there appeared,
   Not e'en a date omitted;
Discrepancies he never feared,
   For everything was fitted.
What quantities of "picks" he used,
   According to the statement!
While "shovel" items you perused,
   Alas, without abatement.

Why thus with repetition mar,
   And like a fool express it?
When — stealings spent at many a bar,
   As Bar Steel who could guess it?
Was ever knave before so silly!
   His wits he should be rallying;
You'd never find in Pic-cadilly,
   Such "pick" a dilly-dallying.

Before directors they were laid,
   And carefully inspected;
For months the scrutiny they made,
   No sign of fraud detected.
At last, of *shovels* and of *picks*
   They heard such frequent mention,
Affairs in this *pick*-uliar fix,
   Demanded some attention.

The matter seemed so very strange,
   That they began to doubt
If rocks upon the mountain-range
   Could really wear them out.
Some said he was a "thieving pup,"
   The veriest of fools;
In view of such a "using up,"
   They wouldn't be his tools!

Of details in regard to drifting,
   They couldn't see the drift;
The *old* machinery he was shifting,
   And with it — he must shift!
Though "blow-outs" and volcanic shocks
   Might indicate a lode,
Ere they for "blow-outs" furnish "rocks,"
   They swear they'll see him blowed!

To be "picked up" by such a "cuss,"
   To be deceived and tricked;
To "shove out" cash for *shovels* thus,
   To have their pockets *picked!*
No wonder then they raved and swore,
   No wonder they abhor him;

Of course, since they had picked a flaw,
    The *picks* were bound to floor him!

Now wasn't this a pretty *pick*-le?
    And yet this handsome knave,
With all his stealings, not a nickel
    Or *pick*-ayune doth save.
With blasted hopes and blemished fame,
    Young CODFISH is distressed;
I'd recommend a change of name,
    And PICK-EREL suggest!

Pray learn from his disastrous end,
    The yawning gulf to shun;
And if you're called to superintend
    A mine for any one;
That none your motives may impeach,
    Should you get in a fix,
Be cautious how you close the breach
    With *shovels* or with *picks!*

A QUERY.

O TRAITORS, cease your "Table Traits!"
"Smart folks eat mustard," you proclaim:
If so, sedate ones live on dates;
That crabbed men eat crabs, is plain,
The peevish, peas, you may avow,
The squabbler, squabs, that I'll allow ·
But tell me, in the name of Cæsar!
If drinking tea will make a teaser?

THE CHEESE BOX.

THE Monitor, the rebels said,
    Was nothing but a cheese box;
The joke was "heavier nor lead"—
    Her rival she with ease knocks.
Her shots went through the Merrimac,
    Their senses grew most flighty;
The cheese was "just the cheese," in fact,—
    They found it most too mite-y!

THE IN-SPIRED AUTHOR.

THE author, friends, of many a pleasing line,
    May pine in sadness on a floor of pine;
In gory alleys write his allegories,
And in an upper story, all his stories.
Compose a fable with af-fable smile,
Upon the crown of what was once a "tile!"
An ode, yet owed for breakfast, all the same,
And mends his pants, although he pants for fame!
Is minus bootjack, so, by Ajax swears;
Takes flights of fancy up four flights of stairs.
Invokes the Muse (mews); result is most appalling,
On yonder wall, the cats keep caterwauling!
If inspiration be the thing desired,
Ascends some lofty spire, and gets in-spired!
Looks through the dingy pane, and is not pained;
In fact it seems a "Paradise Regained."
You ask, why this impression he receives,—
Because he's looking on so many eaves!

DECIDEDLY SHEEPISH!

WHEN mutton falls so low in price,
　　That e'en the poor can buy it,
The butchers wear chop-fallen looks;
　Will any one deny it?

YOUTH — DIVESTED OF SENTIMENT.

LIGHT-HEARTED youth, the season of rare sport,
With pleasing memories thou art ever fraught!
Those gladsome days we all remember well,
Renowned for many a joke and glorious sell;
When urchins roared to see the vigorous kicks
Bestowed on hats profusely lined with bricks!
Delighted saw a miser downward spring,
When quarters vanished by a hidden string!
While snares from lamp-post to the neighboring wall,
Took off tall beavers like a sudden squall!
How fat men swore, who stooped upon the walk,
To pick up letters that were made of chalk!
Or, in the dusky eve, dead rats propelled
By unseen threads, the passer-by beheld;
In vain he raised aloft the ponderous cane,
To strike the "varmint" ere it reached the lane,
Where youthful scamps in force were wont to rally,
Secluded precinct known as DEAD CAT ALLEY.

EPIGRAM ON GORMANDIZER.

A GLORIOUS vision swam before my eyes;
I saw a table groan beneath supplies
Of oysters, ices, jellies, cakes, and pies.
Says I, "What mortal man could these devour
In half a life-time, were his gastric power
E'en like a whale or mastodon?" That hour
Came Gormandizer, sank into a seat
Before that pile, so tempting and so sweet;
I looked — ye gods! the havoc was complete!

JESTING AND DIGESTING.

WE'RE no longer secure; you have seen through our cloaks,
And discovered the secret of making our jokes.
You have peeped through the keyhole, when we have been drinking
A whole tumbler of vinegar, e'en without winking!
You have guessed that our smartness was caused by the tons
Of strong mustard consumed by the makers of puns!
And that all our sharp sayings, the pride of our lives,
Have resulted directly from razors and knives!
Then to follow your reasoning, my friends, to its source,
He who swallows a spoon, is a "spooney," of course!
Yes, the secret is out, your deduction is true;
Let the early reformers pass under review;
For *tall preaching*, pray learn what the stomach requires,
From the Protest they made — at the DIET OF SPIRES!

ON THE DEFENSIVE.

To those who plead for sober, serious thought,
 And on us punsters wage their fierce onslaught,
I'd say a word,—puns old or new advance,
And with these dullards break a friendly lance.
Dramatic men not always take their drams,
Nor clamorous men are found to feed on clams!
Lo! masons are not always "perfect bricks,"
And lumbermen are sometimes merely sticks!
E'en bakers do not show themselves well-bred,
While wicked cobblers harden soles, 'tis said.
Yet should a grocer's conduct be deemed gross,
When jokers often are not found jocose?
Do gamblers only ever "raise the deuce?"
Are tailors always "sound upon the goose?"
Or, is "sheer carelessness" their only feature?
A stylish barber, too, a barbarous creature?
Are fishermen a sort of sel-fish clan?
A man of muscle, friends, a Mussulman?
Confectioners such very candid men?
Should they be pensive who thus wield the pen?

VERY CHAGRINING!

EACH jealous thought I'll drive away,
  Her love I'm sure of winning;
But yet, Sal grinning in a shay,
  I vow is most cha-grining!

IN FOR FUN.

WITH faces long as any moral code,
    View Fun's opponents, who obstruct the road
To true enjoyment, healthful sport, and glee;
To whom a laugh's a crime of high degree.
Time spent in pleasure is time lost, say they,
For "Time is money;" "Better work than play."
All right, my sober friends, but I'm afraid
That I can knock your doctrine in the shade!
Yes, "Time is money," logic most sublime,
But then with *money* can't we have our *time?*
Give me good natured, jolly sort of folks,
Whose ribs are tickled by sharp-pointed jokes;
Whose sides collapse with boisterous, joyous mirth;
Who think there's care enough upon the earth;
That he's a benefactor to his race
Who starts a smile upon a troubled face.
Here's to the chap! whate'er his name or station,
Unknown or honored, of whatever nation,
Who first got up that sovereign cure for fidgets —
The human nose adorned with twirling digits!
Though Mrs. Grundy 'gan to storm and fret,
He stood unmoved and twirled a second set!
She tried to scowl, the effort was in vain;
She bit her lips her laughter to restrain;
Convulsively she turned upon her heel —
Mirth's thunders burst in one terrific peal!
Hooks, eyes, and buttons in their onward flight,
Had reached the street, but for the window-light!

ON THE PROSPECT OF A DRAFT IN NEW YORK CITY.

FIRST, there was Muggins, who was thought quite young,
His dashing style the theme of every tongue;
His fierce moustache and "fighting cut" of hair
Was surely something *a la militaire.*
Such was the braggart swell who daily quaffed
From Pleasure's brim; and yet the call to draft,
Had been in print scarce twenty hours at most,
Before our hero of *old age* could boast!
His stylish dress dilapidated grew,
False teeth were minus, and a glass eye too;
Wig with "transparent parting" laid aside,
Moustache and whiskers were no longer dyed.
Thus nobly sacrificed to war's alarms
Not life, but that which life-like seemed — his charms!
Next there was Stout, and with him many score
Who ate their rations, and could soundly snore;
Yet all at once with divers ills beset,
Lame, halt, and blind, mere skeletons, you bet!
Humpbacked, knock-kneed, consumptive sort of creatures
(Especially at meal time, watch their features)!
O'er such a lengthy list we cannot linger;
Please note the chap who lately lost a finger!

White livered souls! about their ills disputing,
When their frail health most sadly needs — recruiting!
'Tis hard, I grant, to treat with due civility,
Those who enlist with GENERAL DEBILITY.

ON HAND!

A SOVEREIGN'S rule is something grand,
    A teacher's rather flat;
Yet urchins who have mischief planned,
    Must yield the *palm* to that!

The wizard's trick one often views,
    Yet cannot understand;
Like one who doth your hand refuse,
    It's only slight of hand!

A man sees double when he's tight,
    The optics will expand;
As on a watch (not late at night!)
    You've seen a second hand!

For beauty's smiles, if you'd contend,
    You must not listless stand;
But put your best *foot* forward, friend,
    If you would win her hand!

On her bewitching charms you dote,
    Till you are quite unmanned;
A small and tapering hand you note,
    Yet take no note of hand!

ON HAND!

With pistol pointed at your head,
  Your life or cash demanded,
You may *hand over* every red —
  And yet it's under-handed!

The laying on of hands — a rite
  Unchristian men may scorn;
Yet like Macduff, whene'er they fight,
  Their hands keep laying on!

In steamboat cabins, many a wreck
  Of fortune might be told;
You hold the best hand in the deck,
  Worst deck hand's in the hold!

If one insult you without cause,
  "Hands off!" he may demand;
Take him *in hand*, without a pause,
  And polish him off-hand!

From hand to mouth, how folks abhor it,
  When on life's shoals they're stranded;
Down in the mouth (and sometimes o'er it!)
  Because they're not fore-handed!

I've shown my *hand;* perchance you've scanned
  My *feat* — that is, of punning:
Your fat friend writes a running hand,
  Just try his hand at running!

And since my hand is in, once more,
  Attention I command;

ON HAND!

In whist you take one hand in four,
    But never four in hand!

I know you're losing patience fast,
    At length I'm at a stand;
The cobbler's hand is on his last,
    My last is still — On Hand!

THE MYSTERY SOLVED.

WITHIN a miner's cabin there were seated round the hearth,
A group of jolly fellows who were bent on fun and mirth;
A talking o'er their prospects and a tossing off their grog,
And spitting at the jet of flame that flickered on the log.
The ashes on the hearth-stone lay some eighteen inches deep,
And called for sweeping censure, or a very thorough sweep!
When all at once the owner rose, and going toward the door,
He soon returned, and in his hand an iron rod he bore;
And straightway to the hearth he went, and in the pile of ashes,
Began to make, what you would call, some very frantic passes!
And much they wondered, why within the flaky depths he sounded,
Until at last a voice exclaimed, "Confusion worse confounded;

You must be drunk or crazy, Bill, what are you doing, man?"

"Why, don't you see, you stupid fool, *I've lost my frying-pan!*"

A DUBIOUS COMMAND.

AN Irish superintendent, he at whom you've often laughed,
Was standing near the opening of a deep and gloomy shaft,
And leaning o'er the windlass, soon he yelled to those below:
"How many of yees down there, b'ys, that's what I'd like to know?"
"There's *five* o' us, yer honor, since O'Brien's gone to sup."
Then spake this son of Erin, "*Let the half o' yees come up!*"

QUIPS, QUIRKS, AND QUIBBLES.

WONDERFUL!

ON Franklin Square young Tommy you'll descry,
   A hawking papers to the passers-by.
I've read of Progress, things most strange and rare,
But ne'er of Tommy hawking "on the square!"

DOGMATICAL DOGGEREL.

The Mayor proclaims that curs must die,
   The act is justly praised,
For when the ma's of dogs are slain,
   New dog-mas won't be raised!

THE REMEDY!

When dogs set up an awful howl,
   Cane nine of canines vicious,
No sorry cur with cur-sory looks,
   Of peace will dare to dish us!

A STRANGE EPITAPH.

A STRANGE epitaph, in this you'll agree,
"Here lies D. C. Fellow, a *felo de se.*"

A PLEASANT PREDICAMENT!

DIDST ever fall upon the crowded pave
Flat on thy back, and not desire to rave?
'Midst peals of laughter, curse the orange-peel;
And while folks grin, O! how chagrined you feel!

THE GREATER THE CRIME THE LESSER THE OFFENSE.

AN EPIGRAM.

THE man who steals a *dollar*, folks assail,
And cry, "A thief! Consign the wretch to jail!"
But if a *million* — in such light 'tis viewed,
A man's not censured, but considered shrewd!

EDIFICATION.

THE mother views her darling boy with pride:
When Eddy says, O fie, she's edi-fied!

EXTREME TENSION.

When ten avoid a danger, ten shun ill;
A muscle stretched, is called a tension, Bill:
When minds are fixed, it is attention still!

ONE POINT IN COMMON!

Though distinctions 'twixt topers and Hindoos are wide,
On the *jug or not* question they're surely allied!

PERTINENT.

Annie writes versions of such poems as Homer's,
Our ani-mad-versions are not misnomers!

THE SKELETON IN AN AMOUR.

How Art contrives to conjure up
    From Nature's odds and ends,
Such sudden metamorphoses,
    One scarcely comprehends.
With Man she takes but little pains,
    And works with half a will;
But gaze on Woman if you'd see
    The triumphs of her skill.

Behold the ground-work of her plan,—
    A shattered human frame,
A skeleton with parchment skin
    Drawn tightly o'er the same;
With toothless jaws and sunken cheeks,
    A bald and shining pate;
No seeming trace of brow or lash,
    The eye hath lost its mate!

Upon the head she claps a wig
    Of most luxuriant hair;
At such a massive "waterfall,"
    O, won't the people stare!
Be not too curious, or you'll find
    Its contents rather shocking:
Within the depths, a chemisette
    Enveloped in a stocking!

THE SKELETON IN AN AMOUR.

From out the vacant orbit, soon
  An eye of glass is staring!
The artificial and the real
  A close resemblance bearing.
The mouth receives a set of teeth,
  With plumpers for the cheeks,
To fill those sunken features out —
  One of her clever freaks.

With "arching brow" and "drooping lash,"
  The lack of each supplies;
Upon the natural eye she pours
  "*Blanque's Lustre for The Eyes.*"
Thin layers of cosmetic paste
  The wrinkles are entombing;
The visage, thanks to chalk and rouge,
  Grows beautiful and blooming.

Upon the flat, consumptive chest,
  She placed her "patent heavers,"
Those "fixings" made to palpitate
  With secret springs and levers!
And when the stays were tightly laced,
  Jove! what a form they made!
These cannot be "degenerate days"
  When women are so stay-ed!

Unto the shrunken nether limbs,
  "False calves" are next applied,
So perfect is each artifice
  Deficiencies to hide!
Word-limb-ners should be careful what
  They venture to repeat;

Enough, the crowning work of Art
  Stands finished and complete.

When costly silks and finery,
  Had decked the graceful form,
The way she " piled on agony,"
  Took all the world by storm!
The gay gallants around her thronged,
  O'erwhelmed her with attention;
She was the envy of the belles,
  Of beaux, the sole contention.

With poetry and sentiment,
  Most feelingly expressed,
A wealthy young aristocrat
  Soon distanced all the rest.
'Twas after such an interview,
  When on the point of leaving;
O, how she glowed with passion's warmth!
  O, how her breast was heaving!

How pleasing to a lover's eyes,
  Emotion such as this!
So he declared his sentiments,
  And softly stole a kiss.
But, hardly had th' enraptured youth
  The question fairly popped,
Before those strange contrivances,
  The deuced "heavers," stopped!

She was completely thunder-struck,
  And lost her self-command;
He caught a glimpse of something like
  A cord within her hand;

And though she pulled with might and main,
  The "fixings" wouldn't work,
In utter desperation, then,
  She gave an awful jerk!

When, lo! the whole contrivance burst
  With a tremendous shock!
'Twas like the springs and wheels let loose
  Within an eight-day clock:
With rattlesnake accompaniment,
  Solos by swarming bees,
A coffee-mill attachment, and
  A jingling bunch of keys!

He thrust his fingers in his ears,
  To stop the frightful din,
He seized his hat and rang the bell
  To call the servants in.
And ever since, society
  Has laid her on the shelf;
She cannot say they slandered her,
  For she *run down* herself!

PRICES CURRENT.

A PUNSTER'S REVERY.

A PRICES CURRENT is one thing,
    The Price of Currants quite another;
The points I make, affecting one,
    Don't touch on "pints" *outside* the other!

In Indigo, it's awful "blue,"
    Inquiry almost ceasing;
In Leather, but few lots were "sole-d,"
    In Wool, the usual "fleecing!"

In Lime, the trade don't seem to "slack,"
    In Nails, it's always "driving;"
All kinds of Spirits "going down,"
    The "holders" past reviving!

In Flour, they're looking for a "rise"
    Upon an (y)eastern lot!
Though Beans last week were bought on "spec,"
    This week they've "gone to *pot!*"

To glance at Hops, the "figures" show
    Some "close transactions" doing;
From "lively movements" now "on foot,"
    There's surely something "brewing!"

PRICES CURRENT.

Fruit seems to be a "raisin'" now,
    Last week 'twern't worth a "fig!"
So "go in lemons," margin, friends
    Or-range-is mighty big!

Tea not so "steep," 'tis growing "weak,"
    Though Butter's deuced "strong!"
Oil Market "light," Lead "heavy" yet,
    Cheese "moving" right along!

No doubt it goes "against the *grain*,"
    When Corn and Wheat are "flat!"
Since Oats are quoted in demand,
    We'll make a note of that!

With Lumber you shall not be "bored,"
    By e'en the faintest rumor;
"Plank" down the cash, with what a smile
    The dealer greets consumer!

Against short dresses Dry Goods men
    Invoke a fierce tirade;
While Hosiery dealers quietly
    Increase their "stock-in'" trade!

Though Hemp holds dealers in "suspense,"
    'Tis not a hanging matter!
Since Powder is a "brightening up,"
    Don't hesitate, but scatter!

CALIFORNIA

PRICES CURRENT.

Fruit seems to be a "raisin'" now,
    Last week 'twern't worth a "fig!"
So "go in lemons," margin, friends
    Or-range-is mighty big!

Tea not so "steep," 'tis growing "weak,"
    Though Butter's deuced "strong!"
Oil Market "light," Lead "heavy" yet,
    Cheese "moving" right along!

No doubt it goes "against the *grain*,"
    When Corn and Wheat are "flat!"
Since Oats are quoted in demand,
    We'll make a note of that!

With Lumber you shall not be "bored,"
    By e'en the faintest rumor;
"Plank" down the cash, with what a smile
    The dealer greets consumer!

Against short dresses Dry Goods men
    Invoke a fierce tirade;
While Hosiery dealers quietly
    Increase their "stock-in'" trade!

Though Hemp holds dealers in "suspense,"
    'Tis not a hanging matter!
Since Powder is a "brightening up,"
    Don't hesitate, but scatter!

CALIFORNIA

SERIOUS AND OCCASIONAL PIECES.

SHADES AND GLEAMS.

WHEN the weary are fainting 'neath burdens of life,
    And their faces are wrinkled with care;
When the bravest are falling in conflict and strife,
    And the dying are murmuring a prayer;
When misfortune has crushed all the hopes of the young,
    And the aged are cursing their days;
When the wail of despair through the hovel has rung,
    And the king in his palace Death slays;
When disease like a vulture has fastened its fangs,
    And the victim is writhing in pain;
From the belfry of Fate now an iron tongue twangs,
    And we're sighing: "All things are in vain."

Not in vain! not in vain are our toils and restraints,
    Not in vain all our struggles for right;
Though dark shadings appear on the picture life paints,
    Yet the shades on the blessings throw light.
There are bright silver linings to clouds as they rise,
    Though they shadow the heart with their wings;
And how soothing when Anguish is uttering her cries,
    The soft music which Hope sweetly sings.
Though the mysteries of life are concealed from our gaze,

And of truth we are ever in quest,
We shall know — when immortals proclaiming His praise,
Bear us upward to mansions of rest.

COLUMBUS.

A LECTURE—POEM.

AS Clio bids the historic vision rise,
  Lo! ancient Palos stands before your eyes.
The silvery mist with vapor-wings outspread,
That late hung hovering o'er its walls, has fled.
The crimson blushes of the clouds betray
The wooing glances of the king of day.
The restless sea, pursued with searching eye,
Eludes our gaze and merges in the sky;
While murmuring near, by gentler breezes fanned,
The sparkling wavelets kiss the pebbly strand.

Gaze there; O sight unequaled e'er before!
For thousands darken, thousands throng that shore;
Expectant each, most anxious to behold
The man whose brilliant genius did unfold
That glorious project, which proclaims the hour
When Truth asserts the grandeur of her power,
And baffles now her most insidious foes,
Whose base intrigues her destined ends oppose.
The hour is laden with this project grand—
Behold, Columbus seeks an unknown land!

A deathly pallor overspreads the face,
As parting, friend clasps friend in fond embrace,

Then hurries off to join that pensive band;
And soon three little ships set sail from land.
O! what emotion throbs those hearts on shore,
For that brave band may never greet them more.
Mark the fond gaze, affection's blurring tear,
As their loved friends, receding, disappear.
'Tis o'er; their hearts this inward prayer express,
That Heaven will crown the effort with success.

Full oft a seaward glance their steps delay,
While slowly sauntering on their homeward way;
As days elapse, the project rashly deem
A vain conjecture, or an idle dream.
While Gossip shakes her head, and says 'tis plain,
They'll come to nought or sink beneath the main.
The chain of Progress — little did they think,
Was wanting yet this one connecting link,
Forged on the anvil of Columbus' mind;
And lengthened thus — another world would bind.

Long years had passed, and faint success had brought,
Since he conceived that great and mighty thought:
Since to the taunting multitude, he hurled
His vast conception of an unknown world.
Spurned as a madman, shunned on every hand,
None, none would listen to his project grand.
With vacant look he paced the crowded street,
Nor saw the smile of scorn with which men greet
Him, who will yet outlive their pomp and pride,
And win from future years a fame world-wide.

Before the courts of kings he oft displayed
His well-formed plans, with earnest pleas for aid.

The rays of hope resplendent now appear,
Anon, the darkest clouds of doubt and fear.
Delays may harass, anxious cares annoy,
Reward of his long toil — a life's employ;
Yet undismayed, undaunted, he pursued
His mighty thought, with effort still renewed;
With touching eloquence, with fervent zeal,
To kings and nobles made his great appeal.

Youth, manhood spent — perplexed from day to day,
While Care's pale hands entwined his hair with gray.
O, what a life was wasting on this thought!
See Genius doomed a fickle monarch's sport!
Prolonged suspense had nearly crazed his brain;
Men called him fool, repulsed him with disdain.
From home and kindred, all that man holds dear,
He turns at length with many a bitter tear,
To seek from strangers what his king denies,
And at their feet bestow the glorious prize.

Success at length the waning cause attends,
The queen herself the generous aid extends;
Her jewels — precious to a woman's eyes,
Pledged to his cause — Truth's noble sacrifice!
Her couriers speed to bid him swift return,
His own loved country shall no longer spurn.
One flashing glance from eyes divinely bright,
Hath saved the cause and checked the wanderer's flight.
In vain to Europe's kings doth Genius bend —
A queen, a woman, proves his only friend!

This glad success o'ertakes him on his way
To other lands, and thus his steps delay.

Faint hope revives — once more he feels that thrill
Shoot through his frame and banish boding ill.
The Past forgotten — its dark clouds float by,
Bright halos gather in the Future's sky;
A smile flits o'er those deepened lines of care,
As to the court his hastening steps repair.
His queen befriends him; nought can now restrain;
His path lies onward o'er the trackless main.

Again doth Fancy hold before the eye
Her bright, pellucid glass, through which descry
Those little ships where dangers dread appall,
And liquid mountains ever rise and fall.
And tossing thus upon the treacherous deep,
Pale Fright draws near, life's currents feebly creep,
An icy pressure gathers round the heart,
And nameless terrors into being start.
View sturdy sailors, strangers to all fear —
Pale is the cheek, the eye betrays a tear.

Thus fades their hope as fades away the land,
And dire confusion spreads among the band;
But brave Columbus cheers each troubled mind
With glowing tales of lands he hopes to find;
Conceals the reckoning from their startled eyes,
And of the truant compass talks most wise.
In present murmurs, plainly he foresees
The rising tempest in the fluttering breeze.
Hear how he reasons in that threatening hour,
To stay the storm increasing in its power.

Onward they sail, while Nature strews the way
With products rare, to light the dying ray

Of hope ; while from the sea bright isles arise,
Whose distant splendors charm their eager eyes.
As they advance, these vanish from their sight,
Creations of the mind, alas! too bright ;
Wrought from the snowy clouds, bedecked with gold,
Where sun-tints bright illumed the fleecy fold.
The chords from which such thrilling rapture rung,
By Disappointment touched — are all unstrung.

The ocean's vast expanse before them lies,
Unknown, unbounded save by arching skies ;
And danger thus attendant, always near,
Inspired the sailors with a frantic fear.
Old superstitions in that trying hour,
Throng back to haunt them with redoubled power.
Half trembling lest some fabled monster rise,
Ope his wide jaws, and flash his fiery eyes,
Awe-struck they gaze; some utter threats most base
While secret schemings lurk in every face.

Murmurs increase, dissatisfaction grew,
Till foul rebellion spread among the crew.
Swarming the deck the mutineers rebel,
Columbus seek and would by force compel.
He urged anew that land would soon be found,
With grand results their efforts would be crowned.
Then bravely said: "Calm all your fears, my band,
Thus far I've ventured to discover land ;
I shall go on until the land is gained,
By Heaven directed and by Heaven sustained."

With direful danger thus the hour was rife,
While some were threatening e'en to take his life.

When Heaven itself did seem to interpose,
The calm soon ended, and the sea uprose.
The freshening breeze sends courage to each heart,
Reason returns, and each performs his part.
The warbler wandering from its island-home,
Flies forth to greet them o'er sea-fields of foam;
They view with joy the visitant draw near,
And list enraptured to its song of cheer.

The indications of approaching land
Are frequent seen by the impatient band.
Meanwhile the sable curtains of the night
With darkness veil each object from their sight.
Arising from the sea are vapors chill,
While all around is hushed, serenely still;
Save now is heard the zephyr's murmuring moan,
Or the wave sobbing for the sunbeam flown.
There 'mid the gloomy stillness of the deep,
O! what a vigil doth Columbus keep.

Exhausted by unceasing toil and care,
He struggles on when brave hearts would despair;
Drives sleep away, the needful rest foregoes,
Unknown to him unconscious sweet repose.
E'en when tired nature claims a partial rest,
His sleep is troubled and his mind oppressed.
Ah! see him now stand leaning o'er the rail;
Weary and weak, his face careworn and pale,
Still watching as each laggard moment flies,
With sad and thoughtful brow and sleepless eyes.

See! through the darkness of the midnight streams
A radiant light, whose bright and flickering beams

With blank astonishment his eyes perceive ;
Nor could his mind conjecture or conceive
This strange delusion, or whate'er it be,
Save some bright star had stooped to kiss the sea.
Lo, now it moves ! his straining eyes dilate ;
What fitful omen now portends his fate ;
What consummation 'waits his cherished plan ?
The light moves on ! thought centres now on Man !

Hours sped on ; from La Pinta in advance,
There came a sound which fired each drooping glance :
Land, Land ! the cry that through the stillness broke,
From dreams of home the startled sleepers woke :
They throng the decks and through the darkness peer,
Their hearts are stirred by mingled hope and fear.
Deceived so often, could it now be true
That land was near, and yet concealed from view ?
O, that the darkness would but fade away !
They anxious wait the slow approach of day.

As floats the thistle-down before the breeze,
So darkest night before the morning flees.
Was ever sight to mortal eyes more grand,
As dawning day revealed the sought-for land ;
There lay the object of their lengthened toil,
Outlined in beauty, clothed with fertile soil ;
Through stately forests robed in vestments green,
The silver streams meander bright between.
A fragrance sweet is wafted on the air,
To smooth the wrinkles of desponding care.

Tumultuous feelings swayed them in that hour,
Joy thrilled their hearts, despair had lost its power.

Now that success had crowned the enterprise,
Repentant tears were glistening in their eyes.
Regret had seized upon the guilty crew,
And they for pardon now entreating sue.
As he forgave their foul and grievous wrong,
What gladsome shouts the merry band prolong,
While visions bright, enraptured they behold,
Of honors, titles, and exhaustless gold.

The sea lay undisturbed in placid grace,
The rising sun was mirrored on its face.
The merry crew to man the boats prepare,
While martial music echoes on the air.
Behold Columbus clad in rich attire,
His careworn face lit up with youthful fire.
The warlike pomp, the weapons fierce descry:
The grand display, the banners waving high.
Their brawny arms ply well the bending oar,
The boats glide onward towards the welcome shore.

Upon the shore the wondering natives throng,
Gaze on the ships, and startled hear the song
Come o'er the waves, as distant voices raise
The joyous tumult of resounding praise.
While in the lazy flapping sails, they view
The snowy wings that cleft the distant blue;
Deeming the white men inmates of the sky,
Borne down to earth from starry realms on high,
They shrink with fear behind the sheltering tree;
The weird-like spectres skim across the sea.

They near the shore, the keels grate on the sand,
From out their midst, one leaps upon the land.

'Tis brave Columbus, first to touch that soil;
Success at length rewards incessant toil.
Prostrate he knelt and kissed the precious ground,
Shed tears of joy, while followers gathered 'round.
The flush of triumph tinged his pallid cheek,
Joy proved too great, in vain he tried to speak;
Emotion throbbed his breast, his senses thrilled,
His life-long project was at length fulfilled!

. . . .

At Palos, months had slowly passed away
Since the small fleet departed from the bay.
Or bad or joyful tidings none had reached their ears,
To increase their grief or soothe their anxious fears.
The mother thought her absent son no more,
And dreamed she saw him 'mid the billows' roar.
The maiden grew more pale; oft from her breast
Escaped the sigh — her lover was at rest.
Now, as she sought the shore, her questioning eyes
Beheld a speck grow larger 'gainst the skies.

And long she watched with breathless silence there —
Love never yet was known to brook despair;
But Hope's low embers still had nursed a spark,
To kindle forth when shrouded in the dark.
Joy lit her eyes and flushed the cheek so pale,
The misty verge disclosed a tiny sail!
Quick spread the news, commotion stirred the town,
With breathless speed vast crowds came hurrying down;
All traffic ceased, the bells with welcome rung,
While shouts of triumph loosed each silent tongue.

No more the prattling dreamer of his age,
The jest of courtier and the scoff of sage;

No more shall children when they him descry,
Point to their foreheads as he passes by.
He triumphs now despite their taunts and jeers,
Solves ocean's mystery for all coming years.
By unborn millions shall his name be blest,
Who opes the pathway to the boundless West.
See! he returns; the precious news he brings,
Shall make him greater e'en than thronèd kings.

The weather-beaten ship, with tattered sails,
Told of fierce conflicts with terrific gales;
When all seemed lost, and when the lightning's glare
Illumined faces livid with despair;
When vows, entreaties, prayers, seemed all in vain,
The tempest's awful fury to restrain;
When fear had seized upon the bravest heart,
Columbus silent stood, from all apart,
With deep emotion gazed around, o'erhead,
Upon the warring elements — all hope had fled!

O, potent hour! for lasting good or ill,
E'en now we seem to see that giant will
Confront his pending fate with dauntless breast,
As boding thoughts his troubled mind oppressed.
Still raged the storm, no pity seemed to show:
His Great Discovery earth may never know,
The fatal surge o'er them engulfing sweep,
And Genius in its depths forever sleep.
His fate unknown, the world Columbus deem,
A fool who perished for an idle dream.

The raging blast was shrieking through the shrouds,
Rain fell in torrents from the inky clouds;

The angry waves upon the deck would crawl,
Dart out their frothy tongues, as if to appall
The trembling wretches clinging to the mast,
As towards the skies imploring looks they cast.
The surging sea more threatening seemed to roll;
Columbus wrote upon a parchment scroll,
Then glanced on high, as 'mid the waves he hurled
The cask that held the record of a world!

Success — the measure of enduring fame;
While failure merits scorn, reproach, and shame.
As Genius struggles towards his destined end,
To one or other all his efforts tend.
A pebble proves no barrier to success,
The towering mountains cause our sole distress.
They rise before us in the paths we tread,
And check our course like phantoms stark and dread.
Thus, had he perished in the stormy haze,
No gentle Irving ere had lisped his praise.

Propitious Heaven ordained the enterprise;
The fearful storm gave place to sunny skies.
Their trials, dangers, and disasters passed,
The little ship is safely moored at last:
Columbus welcomed now with loud acclaim,
By those who once had been the first to blame,
Whose cruel schemes were planned in vain to thwart
The glorious object which Columbus sought.
Ovations greet him now on every hand, —
The Great Discoverer of another land!

Loud in his praise was Gossip's nimble tongue,
Age felt new life, wild transports thrilled the young.
The Old World, all that ever met their view —
It paled before the splendors of the New,
Whose dazzling glories were as yet untold,
Whose crystal streams were bright with glistening gold.
Lo! countless thousands now his pathway throng,
With loud huzzas and glorious bursts of song.
His king receives him with most gracious mien;
How great his triumph and how grand the scene!

. . . .

Turn from the pageant, stop the trumpet's breath;
The scene is changed, it is the hour of death.
O Genius, what a cruel fate is thine!
Though base Injustice left thee thus to pine,
Though cold Ingratitude rewards thy pains,
And Envy bound thy aged limbs with chains,
Though brazen Fraud, unto his lasting shame,
Hath robbed a world of its discoverer's name —
Wherever Truth and Justice are revered,
To every breast thy name shall be endeared —

The minstrel wake from his inspiring dream,
And seek in vain to find a nobler theme.
The page of history with thy name shall blaze,
Proclaim thy struggles and enhance thy praise.
Youth shall a lesson from thy greatness learn,
And struggle onward though the world should spurn;
The voice of eloquence thy story tell,
The hearts of thousands with emotion swell.

Honor for thee shall wake the trembling lyre,
Fame write her scroll in characters of fire.

O heartless Ferdinand! thou didst repay
A life of hardship with unjust delay.
When sickness laid him low, in vain he sues
His king to grant him but his promised dues.
With cold neglect thou answerest all his prayers,
Withhold'st the pittance for his toils and cares
Though he was dying! O, what lasting scorn
Awaits thee from the millions yet unborn!
His world-wide fame no sceptered king can blast,
On Time's great wheel Truth topmost stands at last.

REMEMBRANCE.

OFTTIMES we're sad, our sky seems overcast
   With stretching clouds, and then we seek re-
   pose
Of mind: at Thought's ethereal touch, unclose
The crystal gates to Memory's hall, so vast.
Radiance streams o'er the pictures of the Past —
   The pictures painted in our lives each day;
   There they remain and will remain alway,
To haunt or please us with their sight at last.
O, what a lesson for our guidance traced:
   A word once spoken, cannot be unsaid,
A deed once done, can never be effaced!
   Let Virtue's coloring o'er each scene be spread,
And let our lives with actions just be graced —
   The Past a halo round our Future shed.

THE SOFT ANSWER.

TREASURES vast we'd scatter wide,
   Could we but renounce
Words of passion and of pride,
   Hasty tongues pronounce —

Words which chafed the hearts of those
   Bound by dearest ties,
Till affection's waters rose
   Gushing from the eyes.

Mould in love thy angry speech,
   Smiles, not frowns display;
For 'tis this, the Scriptures teach,
   Turneth wrath away.

THE TAUNT.

How many ne'er had erred
    But for the taunting word,
  That wrought its spell;
This was the fatal sting,
This shot broke virtue's wing,
    Earthward they fell.

The taunt that cleft the air
Dispelled a mother's prayer
    Some heart had cherished;
The parted lips would speak,
But blushes tinged the cheek —
    The "No!" had perished.

O! taunt not those who aim
To live without a blame —
    Withhold the blow;
Else, see thy victim fall,
And plunge beyond recall,
    In deepest woe.

O YOU MAY SING OF THE ROSY WINE.

A TEMPERANCE DITTY.

O YOU may sing of the rosy wine,
    As its sparkling bubbles rise,
And sip its sweets as a gift divine,
    Till its blush is in your eyes.

But think, my friends, of the woe it brings
    To the hearts of old and young—
Its taste has flown on the vision's wings,
    And the song remains unsung.

If all could drink with the reason clear,
    With the mind undimmed and sound,
O, then Life's bark would have nought to fear
    From the rocks that rise around.

'Tis sad to think that the noblest heart
    Is the first ofttimes to fall;
In vain the tears of a mother start,
    And in vain her lips may call.

The wine-stream flows with its rosy face
    On the heart so pure and fair,
Engraved with truth and each gentle grace—
    Till it wears the record bare!

THE WAR.

As the lightning's instant stroke
    Shivers heart of rugged oak,
Through the battle's stifling smoke
    Belching cannons flash.
Shouts of triumph, banners flying;
Groans and shrieks of thousands dying;
See the ghastly faces lying —
    Hear the weapons clash!

Fierce the conflict now is raging,
Hand to hand the foe engaging:
Death, destruction, each is waging,
    As the columns meet.
See the eyes with hatred glaring!
See the looks of those despairing!
See the ponderous missiles tearing
    Ranks now incomplete!

List the widow's lonely sighing;
Hear the frantic maiden crying
For her lover, wounded, dying;
    See the mother's grief!
God! O spare our Country's life;
If through bloody, civil strife,
With fresh horrors make it rife,
    That it may be brief.

THE PROPHET OF OUR DREAMS.

BENEATH a cowl of roses, odorous with a rich perfume,
With noiseless step, the prophet Hope invades the silent room,
And on our sad and heavy heart he breathes a witching spell;
The ear drinks in sweet music, as the murmur of a shell;
Bright visions flit across the mind — in vain it strives to seize,
We're borne away on downy wings and lost in reveries.
Ah! then he whispers thrilling words, and lifts the cowl of roses —
A face of beauty, lit with smiles, unto our gaze discloses.
We list enraptured to the words that tell our future fate —
On us the eyes of beauty shine, on us the proudest wait.
We see an airy castle rise, its crystal gates behold;
We dream of fame, and honor's prize, and clutch at hoards of gold.
We hear again the wierd-like strain that murmurs soft and low:
We see the silver lining to the sombre cloud of woe.

The mind awakes to living things, the senses wildly thrill;
The prophet has departed, and the room is silent still.
Begone, false prophet! shout we, and forever quit our sight —
Yet stay! thy visions haunt us yet, and fill us with delight.
As through the murky darkness now we strain our eager eyes,
We see a flitting shadow pause, and point us to the skies.

POEM

FOR THE FOURTH OF JULY CELEBRATION AT DENVER, COLORADO, 1865.

DARKLY the clouds were obscuring our vision,
    Chilling our hopes and awakening our fears;
Stony-faced Fate, how we braved thy decision,
    When the first war-note had startled our ears!
When sister stars from our firmament straying,
    Threatened destruction and death to our land,
Hatred the breast of our brother was swaying —
    Reason no longer had power to command.

Then the great North like a giant was shaken,
    Buckling its armor for conflict and strife;
Turning not back from the path it had taken,
    Battling for Union and national life:
Fighting the same bloody conflict of ages,
    Which through the annals of history we scan;
Solving the problem which puzzled the sages —
    Freedom the birthright of God unto man!

Breaking the chain which to error had bound us,
    Crushing the viper we warmed into life;
Vowing that slavery no more should confound us,
    Breeding its factions and sectional strife.
But when redeemed from the curse that hung o'er us,
    We, as a people, united should stand —

Lo! what a prospect would open before us,
   When the great Future should dawn on our land.

Fierce was the struggle, and bloody, and long,
   Greater than ever the world had beheld;
Armies so mighty, a people so strong,
   Tempests of fury so slow to be quelled.
In the great balance the Nation oft trembled,
   Often the pulse of the people beat low;
Strong in their cause were the sons, who resembled
   Fathers whose footsteps once crimsoned the snow!

All the old monarchs of Europe grew stronger,—
   Stronger in hope of their tenure of power;
Deeming our Nation a Nation no longer,
   That, in the contest, at length we must cower;
Going the way of Republics before us,
   Into the depths of oblivion's sea;
But, on this day — lo! the Nation's grand chorus
   Thunders the answer — To-day we are free!

Slowly the years round the dial were creeping,
   Bringing the struggle at length to a close;
Southward the army of Sherman was sweeping,
   Striking rebellion most terrible blows.
Onward, towards Richmond, our heroes were routing
   Lee and the rebels who held us at bay;
Sherman and Grant! — lo! the people are shouting,
   Proudly o'er Richmond our flag floats to-day!

From the dark cloud, lo! the sunlight was streaming,
   Faint was the echo from War's brazen throat;
Joy in the face of the Nation was beaming,
   Justice the cause of the traitor had smote.

POEM FOR THE FOURTH OF JULY.

Out from the cloud with its golden-hued splendor,
    Shot the swift thunderbolt, crazing our brain;
He whom you loved, so kind-hearted and tender,
    LINCOLN — the hope of the people — was slain.

Fell was the blow which had startled the nation,
    Hellish the plot which assassins had planned;
Striking at those who were highest in station,
    Shrouding in sorrow the hopes of the land.
Breakers of chaos around us were roaring,
    Threatening the old Ship of State to o'erwhelm;
Shades of the heroes above us were soaring,
    God of our fathers was guiding the helm!

Out of the furnace of trial the stronger,
    Out of the shadow and into the sun;
Shaken with war and convulsion no longer,
    Freedom has triumphed, the battle is won!
Honor the heroes — for us they have bled,
    Green be the turf o'er each patriot's grave;
Honor the living, and honor the dead.
    Long as the flag they have rescued shall wave!

Tendril and vine from the bomb-shell is springing,
    And the old battle-fields blossom with beauty!
Peace is the anthem which Nature is singing,
    Plant the fresh germs of affection and duty.
Pardon the foe and bring back the old feeling,
    Rebels are shedding the tears of regret;
As round the altar of Country we're kneeling,
    Charity whispers — "Forgive and forget."

Into the sunlight again we are drifting,
    Darkness and sorrow like shadows have flown;
Hope — the dim veil of the Future is lifting,
    Glimpses of glory around us are thrown.
Banish the Past, for the pathway before us
    Leads to a Future most dazzling and grand;
Borne on her snowy wings Peace hovers o'er us,
    Rainbows of Promise encircle the land.

POEM

FOR THE MASONIC CELEBRATION AT DENVER, COLORADO,
JUNE 24, 1867.

RING out the song of gladness, let the glorious pæan swell,
In going round the Circle, we have touched the Parallel!
The day the old sun-worshippers in ages past revered,
By stronger ties of sympathy to Masons is endeared.
To-day, the faithful everywhere, who work by Square and Line,
Shall hail the blessed memory of our patron saint divine.

The Beauteous Column stands erect — no work laid out to-day,
From labor to refreshment, we the welcome call obey.
The 'Prentice in the quarry's depths no Ashlar Rough shall bear,
The Craftsman lay aside his tools — the Level, Plumb, and Square;
The Master Workman on the wall, delay the Grand Design —
To hail the blessed memory of our patron saint divine.

Throughout the nation, far and wide, the mystic legions throng,
Firm champions in the cause of truth, the secret foes of wrong.
Each quiet hamlet echoes with the sound of tramping feet;
They move in mighty concourse through the city's crowded street;
Their banners waving proudly, while their jewels brightly shine,
In honor of the memory of our patron saint divine.

No blood-stained laurels deck the brows of that fraternal band,
No desolation marks their path, no ruins strew the land;
Their victories are o'er sin and wrong, o'er suffering, want, and pain,
Ascending prayers of gratitude their sweetest bugle strain,
As round the crushed and bleeding heart love's tendrils they entwine —
Those who thus hail the memory of their patron saint divine.

The pure and spotless lambskin is the glorious badge they wear;
They wage their moral warfare with the Compass and the Square.
The upraised hand is paralyzed, and passion stricken dumb,
For each must walk uprightly with his eye upon the Plumb —

Those brethren of the mystic tie, whose hearts this day incline,
To celebrate the memory of our patron saint divine.

Then usher in our gala day with joyousness and mirth,
And swell the grand old chorus as it circles round the earth,
With kindly words of greeting from the mountains to the sea —
Our hearts are on the Level, though our bodies may not be ;
Then gathering round the festive board, pour forth the generous wine,
And drink a toast in memory of our patron saint divine.

'Tis fitting on a day like this, when brethren thus are met,
To dwell on themes each Mason loves and never can forget ;
To trace the course of Masonry until it disappears
Amid the ruins of the past, the gathering gloom of years,
Till breaking through the mists of time, it bursts upon our sight,
And pours from Mount Moriah's hill, its blazing stream of light.

Coeval with creation though its truths illumed the earth,
'Twas in the reign of Solomon our Order had its birth.
Among the thousands of the Craft who at the Temple wrought,
It stamped its mighty impress on each action, word, and thought.

Two Temples they were rearing by the aid of Square and Line,
The Outward and Material — the Inward and Divine.

The One — in silent grandeur rose; no ringing sound was heard
Of axe or other metal tool, nor one discordant word.
In perfect peace and harmony they plied their cunning art,
The secret tie of Brotherhood had bound them heart to heart.
And lo! the toiling legions from the Quarry to the Hill,
Were moved by its mysterious power and felt its quickening thrill.

Seven years they wrought with patient toil, and when their work was done,
The Temple with its golden spires stood glistening in the sun.
Its splendor and magnificence enraptured every gaze,
And filled the thronging multitudes with wonder and amaze.
As Israel's crowning glory shall its fame forever last,
And in Tradition's whispers link the present to the past.

The Other — when the eyes wax dim, and fainter grows each breath,
Approaches its completion and awaits the Capestone — Death.
If mystic tools and implements, and symbols pure and bright

Have served their holy purpose and have fashioned it aright —
The Temple of a Glorious Life stands finished and complete,
And in that Foreign Country with the Builder we shall meet.

The Temple of King Solomon completed 'neath their hands,
The Craft dispersed and wandered forth through earth's remotest lands.
They heard the Gavel echo and they saw the Trowel gleam,
Amid Arabia's deserts and by Egypt's sacred stream.
They crossed the plains of Syria, the mountains of Judæa,
In Asia and in India they were scattered far and near.

Within the silent wilderness, and on the desert waste,
The relics of their genius are amid the ruins traced.
They reared earth's grandest monuments, her temples and her fanes;
Alas! 'neath Time's unsparing hand — scarce one of them remains.
Before the Chaldee's vengeful ire, the Temple was o'erthrown,
The gorgeous fabric sank to earth, a shapeless mass of stone.

The Temple made of wood and stone may crumble and decay,
But there's a viewless fabric which shall never fade away.

Age after age each Mason strives to carry out the plan,
But still the work's unfinished which those ancient Three began.
None but immortal eyes may view complete in all its parts,
The Temple formed of Living Stones — the structure made of hearts.

Although the Craft for centuries is often lost to view,
Within the darkest ages they were steadfast, firm, and true.
Despite the dungeon and the rack, relentless bigots failed
To penetrate the mystery with which our truths were veiled;
Within the hidden caves of earth, secure from lurking foes,
The hallowed lights still burned undimmed, the clouds of incense rose.

'Neath every form of government, in every age and clime,
Amid the world's convulsions and the ghastly wrecks of time,
While empires rise in splendor and are conquered and o'erthrown,
And cities crumble in the dust, their very sites unknown,
Beneath the sunny smile of peace, the threatening frown of strife,
Lo! Masonry has stood unmoved — with age renewed her life.

She claims her votaries in all climes, for none are under ban,
Who place implicit trust in God, and love their fellow-man.
The heart that shares another's woe, beats just as warm and true,
Within the breast of Christian, or Mohammedan, or Jew.
She levels all distinctions from the highest to the least,
The King must yield obedience to the peasant in the East.

When troubles come, as come they must, and fortune wears a frown,
The cruel world will shun a man the moment he is down.
Behold the Mason's hand outstretched, his eyes with tears are wet,
He'll lift him to his feet again, he is a brother yet.
The Mason finds, whate'er his lot, where'er his footsteps roam,
"In every clime a brother, and in every land a home."

Dear ladies! though our rites are veiled, our secrets hid from view,
There is a chord within our hearts which binds us unto you.
Through husband, father, brother, you to us may be allied,
In sickness, trouble, or distress, your wants be satisfied.

Should tempter with his arts assail, or dangers dread alarm.
As long as there's a Mason near, you shall not suffer harm.

Though countless rites and mysteries have sought to sway mankind,
To make their impress on the heart, or captivate the mind,
Yet Masonry survives them all, the undistinguished crowd —
She saw them in their swaddling-clothes and in their burial shroud;
The new-born truths they fain would teach, and which they built upon,
Were scattered rays from Masonry — the blazing central sun.

Let those who rail at Secrecy, pray tell us what is Life,
The greatest mystery yet unsolved, although with theories rife;
Why God, the Mighty Builder, veils his purposes from view;
Why Nature teems with labyrinths, we grope and wander through.
God's hallowed truths, to us revealed, the basis of our art,
Are hidden from the vulgar gaze and graven on the heart.

The Temple of the Universe, which God himself hath made,
With what a grand mosaic is its beauteous pavement laid.

POEM FOR ST. JOHN'S DAY.

Tall mountains with cloud-chapiters, the fabric rests upon,
Roofed with the blue ethereal sky, illumined by the sun.
'Mid songs of birds and murmuring streams, and thunders deep and loud,
The novice makes his progress from the cradle to the shroud.

What honored names on history's page, o'er whose brave deeds we pore,
Have knelt before our sacred shrine, and trod the checkered floor.
Kings, princes, statesmen, heroes, bards, who squared their actions true,
Between the Pillars of the Porch, they pass in long review.
O brothers! what a glorious thought for us to dwell upon;
The Mystic Tie which binds our hearts, bound that of WASHINGTON.

Although our past achievements we with conscious pride review,
As long as there's Rough Ashlars, there is work for us to do.
We still must shape the Living Stones with instruments of love,
For that eternal Mansion in the Paradise above,
Toil as we've toiled in ages past, to carry out the plan —
'Tis this: The *Fatherhood* of GOD, the *Brotherhood* of MAN.

NOTES.

Note 1, page 52. — Immense numbers from South Bend and Posey County, Indiana, also from Pike County, Missouri, helped to swell the tide of emigration to the gold regions.

Note 2, page 52. — "Prairie schooner." A large emigrant or freight wagon.

Note 3, page 56. — "Color." The residue of small particles of gold remaining in the pan, after the dirt has been washed or "panned out."

Note 4, page 58. — "Graybacks." Body lice of a large size, and of a grayish color. No allusion would have been made to such disgusting objects, were it not for the attention they have received at the *hands* of thousands!

Note 5, page 59. — "To make the riffle." Literally, to achieve success.

Note 6, page 59. — "A man for breakfast." An expression signifying that a murder has been committed.

Note 7, page 59. — "Vigys." Members of the Vigilance Committee.

Note 8, page 61. — "Muckie-muck." Of Indian origin, signifying "last resource."

Note 9, page 65. — Pronounced War-for-no, or War-fa-nor.

Note 10, page 65. — "Bummer." An individual who was never known to miss a meal or pay a cent.

Note 11, page 65. — "Caravan." An affair resembling a cage for wild beasts, used for transporting express matter across the plains.

www.ingramcontent.com/pod-product-compliance
Lightning Source LLC
Chambersburg PA
CBHW020057170426
43199CB00009B/314